Donald Dreyfuss
Austin, Texas
Dec. 1986

THE ETHIC OF TIME

Wylie Sypher

THE ETHIC OF TIME
Structures of Experience in Shakespeare

A CONTINUUM BOOK

THE SEABURY PRESS · NEW YORK

1976
The Seabury Press
815 Second Avenue, New York, New York 10017

An abbreviated version of Chapter IX appeared in *The Structurist* (No. 15/16, Fall,
1975–6), as "Space and Time in Renaissance Painting and Drama," and grateful
acknowledgment is made to that journal.

Printed in the United States of America

LIBRARY OF CONGRESS CATALOGING IN PUBLICATION DATA

Sypher, Wylie.   The ethic of time.
(A Continuum book)   Bibliography: p. 211
1. Shakespeare, William, 1564–1616—Criticism and interpretation. 2. Time in
literature. I. Title.
PR3069.T5S9   822.3'3   76–13844   ISBN 0–8164–9299–9

To the members of the
Simmons College Department of English,
who have been abiding friends

"Every age, so far at any rate, has been able to find in Shakespeare whatever it needed to maintain contact with him . . ."

Frank Kermode: Shakespeare, Spenser, Donne

"The business of Shakespeare criticism would have no point if it were not necessary to re-read him to suit the always-changing interests of the times."

Andrew Gurr: The Shakespearean Stage, 1574–1642

"It is notorious that Shakespeare would not understand much modern Shakespearean criticism. But then that, in itself, is hardly an objection to what the critics are doing. Newton, equally, would presumably not understand modern physics."

George Watson: The Study of Literature

Contents

Preface

In his essay on "Tradition and the Individual Talent" T. S. Eliot quotes "someone" who said that "the dead writers are remote from us because we *know* so much more than they did." But this judgment does not fully apply to Shakespeare—or at least it applies less to Shakespeare than to almost any other writer. Shakespeare's overwhelming comprehension makes him abidingly modern, capable of perpetual resurrection in light of what we may increasingly "know." In his own way he seems to have "known" what we have merely rephrased in our own fashion and language. Although it is a vulgarism to "explain" any of the plays by our current clinical or scientific theories, Shakespeare's astonishing intuition leads us continuously to re-read the plays with a sustained awareness of their relevance to what we "know," or think we know. Thus our interpretations constantly expand.

This expanded understanding does not nullify any interpretation of Shakespeare as an Elizabethan, and we need to know all we possibly can about the Renaissance mentality even if we cannot fully recover the cast of that mentality. So there are two valid means of interpreting Shakespeare: as an Elizabethan, and as a writer who transcends the Elizabethan mentality. Shakespeare is classic in the sense that he constantly affords us new meanings, is always alive to

modern consciousness. Thus there are "correct" or war-
ranted interpretations of the Elizabethan meanings in the
plays, though we are also able to superimpose upon these
undeniable meanings others that reach beyond the day
when the plays were written and first acted.

It is clear, as Ricardo J. Quinones has said in his recent
book, *The Renaissance Discovery of Time*, that "for the men of
the Renaissance, time is a great discovery." But not only for
Renaissance man, since time is a basic enigma in our current science, philosophy, and ethic, and there is now a vast
range of provocative theory devoted to the nature of time
and to our differing modes of consciousness of time. The
scope and complexity of the time problem in modern
thought are suggested in J. T. Fraser's huge anthology, *The
Voices of Time*, a collection on which I have heavily relied.
A great many of its pages, written by scientists, invite us,
by hindsight, to reconsider what happens in Shakespearean
drama. Indeed, Shakespeare, in his oft-obsessive concern
with time, appears intuitively to have anticipated many of
our divergent views of the nature and meaning of our experience of time. Many of the sonnets verify how deeply
Shakespeare, like any Renaissance man, was fascinated and
troubled by the dilemmas of time, but a fuller expression
of these dilemmas can be found in the plays.

If the Fraser anthology indicates that we ourselves have
no one coherent interpretation of time, the Shakespearean
dramas, even more than the sonnets, indicate that, like us,
Shakespeare could not rely upon any single conception of
time. His consciousness of the time experience is multiple,
the various aspects and forms of this time experience being
inherent in play after play. The miracle is that Shakespeare
seems to have understood so much about so many of the
ways in which time manifests itself to man. In the Fraser
anthology the name of Henri Bergson, that subtle modern
philosopher of time, often recurs. So I have not hesitated
to invoke Bergson, although Bergson has of late been
deemed vulnerable.

The problem of time in recent thought has been associated intimately with problems of space, and I trust that my final chapter, which comments upon spatial consciousness, will be found pertinent even if we have lost the Renaissance vision of Arcadian realms.

My debts to numberless writers are suggested—and merely suggested—in my passing references or in the notes, and I must specify how much I owe to critics like Maynard Mack, Ricardo J. Quinones, Hallett Smith, Frederick Turner, Emrys Jones, Mark Rose, Georges Poulet, Tom F. Driver, E. M. W. Tillyard, Jacqueline de Romilly, Gaston Bachelard, Rudolf Wittkower, Gaston Roupnel, Kenneth Clark, Irving Ribner, Norman Rabkin, G. Wilson Knight, R. G. Collingwood, Frank Kermode, Jean Pucelle, and Anton Ehrenzweig. Many of them, no doubt, would have reservations about what I have tried to say.

Above all I am especially obligated to Justus George Lawler, who as editor so intelligently, understandingly, and graciously suggested changes in the manuscript; and to Margot Shields for all her care and good will in guiding the book through publication.

I
The Measures of Time:
Four Time Schemes

Anthropologists tell us that every culture has its own time sense. Primitive societies seem to have no sense of progressive historical time since for them time is seasonal, a recurrent cycle of birth, death, and rebirth. This archaic time sense is closely associated with fertility ceremonies, and behind these rituals is an abiding faith in renewal—the past will recur as the future. But for the historical view, the past is gone and the future will be unlike the past. As Norman O. Brown remarks, "Archaic time is cyclical, periodic, unhistoric: modern time is progressive (historical), continuous, irreversible."

The contrast between cyclic and historical views of time became apparent in Greek experience, which was a transition from the archaic to the modern mentality. This transition expressed itself in tragedy, a form of art that is seasonal or ceremonial in origin, but is also filled with a sense of the irreversibility of the past. Northrop Frye has said, "The basis of the tragic vision is being in time, the sense of the one-directional quality of life, where everything happens once and for all, where every act brings unavoidable and fateful consequences, and where all experience vanishes, not simply into the past, but into nothingness, annihilation." Yet their heritage of primitive thought suggested to the Greeks that they lived in a universal order governed by a regular rhythm, an alternation of season symbolizing eternal law. The chthonic and mystery cults were deeply tinged by this rather primitive sense of *Aion* or sacred time, which is ahistoric, perhaps ultimately oriental.

With the onset of the tragic view there came a new consciousness of the relation between past and future and the fatality of acts done whose consequences could not be foreseen, yet were inescapable. Over against the notion of *Aion* there came a sense of *Chronos,* the time of history or fortune, and the plays of the three great dramatists disclose the inconsistencies in the Greek apprehension of time.

In her discussion of *Time in Greek Tragedy,* Jacqueline de Romilly identifies three competing time schemes in Aeschylus, Sophocles, and Euripides, showing how the Greeks, under stress, were living in a new atmosphere of instability, uncertainty, perhaps confusion. Aeschylus assigns time an ethical meaning, for time brings retribution, the penalties required by a moral dispensation inherent in the cosmos, called *moira, nemesis,* or *diké.* Sophocles, on the contrary, seems closer to Heraclitus, intimating that time is not so much an agent of justice as an evidence of the insecurity of life. With his submerged pessimism Sophocles undermines Aeschylean piety, suggesting that disaster befalls one who cannot adapt himself, because of obstinacy, to the changing demands of his existence. Sophoclean time is a threat to the one who stands out against *pankrates chronos.* The Sophoclean figure exists in "anxious waiting" for a future that is more menacing than it is in Aeschylus.

Finally, in Euripides, time becomes an aspect of the debilitating casualties in life, and the tragic figure falls victim to mere chance, events, fortune, *tyche.* This means that the Euripidean character has a diminished heroism, for he exists at a pitch of apprehension, a new self-awareness springing from restlessness, rebellion, fear, or self-distrust. The Euripidean women, especially, feel the bitter contrast between the safety of the past and the threat of misfortune; they are thrown back upon memory with a pathos that is nearly Proustian.

In short, there is no such thing as "the" Greek sense of time; there are mainly, as in *Hamlet,* times out of joint. R. G. Collingwood detects in Greek historiography a similar discord between a quest for the eternal or timeless and the new sense of the episodic. The Greeks, too, suffered from a dissociation of sensibility, and Nietzsche justly notes that they were equipped for suffering precisely because the shining fantasy of the Olympian order did not ease the foreboding in their lives.

These inconsistencies, with their attendant insecurity, are relevant to the Elizabethan mentality with its disturbing sense of mutability, which shook faith in the stability of a world order. Greek and Elizabethan playwrights alike indicate that drama thrives on uncertainties in ages when the foundations of belief have been unsettled, when there are competing readings of experience, when logic has reached a point of diminishing returns. There is a Euripidean tone in Elizabethan theatre, and one evidence of the Elizabethan mentality of crisis, as Hardin Craig once called it, is this dread of mutability. Spenser has a sense of the peril in *Chronos,* the fell hand of time lying heavily on Shakespeare's sonnets as well as on *The Faerie Queene,* making the opening of the Mutability cantos almost a cry of despair:

> What man that sees the ever-whirling wheele
> Of Change, the which all mortall things doth sway,
> But that thereby doth find, and plainly feele,
> How Mutability in them doth play
> Her cruell sports, to many mens decay?

We speak of the Elizabethan world order, but there was also a disorder. Clifford Leech has written of the Elizabethans what would also be true of the age of Sophocles and Euripides:

Standing between a belief in natural order and a growing perception of chaos, between the Renaissance enthusiasm for living and an ever-darkening disillusion, between the twin poles of Fate and Chance, of predestination and free will, they went through mental experiences of a peculiar intensity, knew the darkness and the terror all the more keenly for the light that still remained in a diminishing fragment of the heavens. And because their feelings were so deeply stirred by the contradictions in their experience, they were led to the writing of tragic literature. *(Shakespeare's Tragedies)*

In these writers "the equilibrium was precarious indeed."

The insecurity in Elizabethan experience is nowhere more evident than in the alternative, even the discordant, views of time in Shakespearean drama. For the time problem in Shakespeare involves much more than the so-called double or stretched theatrical anachronism mentioned by Thomas Rymer, and the task of redeeming the time is in many plays deeply related to the dilemma of reconciling the moral and political orders, and with taking arms against a sea of troubles.[1]

The history plays, and notably *Richard III*, are a convenient means of approaching the complexity of Shakespearean time, or, more accurately, the diverse time schemes that were like unexamined premises. Clifford Leech has grouped these diverse time schemes: the experience of time as cyclic and the experience of time as crisis.[2] *Richard III*, with its radically different time schemes, is among the problematic manifestations of the Elizabethan uncertainty about the meaning of history.

To identify these meanings, I shall be arbitrary in specifying four unlike, or at least distinguishable, conceptions of time. *Richard III*, offering a paradigm of these different conceptions, has a kind of quadruple movement, shifting as it does between simple chronicle, the cycle of Fortune, a nearly Aeschylean time of retribution, and moments of psychic duration.

The first conception of time is purely sequential or linear, one that makes no attempt to derive any meaning of time beyond a merely chronological succession of events. This mere chronometric succession, literally an annal, has none of the significance attaching to the idea of mutability. In this simple time sequence the episode stands out in isolation without any halo of psychic or dramatic implication. In its plainest form this merely linear time sense of the "factual" annal is represented by a document like the *Anglo-Saxon Chronicle*, which records, without dramatic accent or emphasis, the series of Danish raids on England year by year:

> 514: In this year the West Saxons came to Britain with three ships at the place called Cedricsora; and Stuf and Wihtgar fought against the British and put them to flight. 519: In this year Cerdic and Cynric seized the Wessex kingdom and in the same year they fought against the British in the place now called Cerdicesford. . . .

This kind of neutral, granular episode occurs in *Richard III* when Gloucester appears in council and suddenly says, with the discontinuity of chronicle:

> My Lord of Ely, when I was last in Holborn
> I saw good strawberries in your garden there.
> I do beseech you send for some of them. (III, 4)

So the strawberries are fetched, an action that has little to do with the business of the scene, which is Richard's malignly sentencing Hastings to quick death.[3] The strawberry episode derives directly from Holinshed's *Chronicle*, where it has more meaning than it does in the play, since it suggests Richard's feigned good humor:

> After a little talking with them, he said unto the bishop of Elie: "My lord, you have verie good strawberries at your garden in Holborn, I require you let us have a messe of them." "Gladlie, my lord" (quoth he) "would God I had some better thing as readie to your pleasure as that!" And

therewithall in all the hast he sent his servant for a messe
of strawberies.

The passage in the play is anecdotal, told in the time
scheme of the annal—an incident that is material for history or drama, but hardly of itself history or drama.

For history, like drama, provides an interpretation of
events. In his essay called "A Few Words," Paul Valéry
remarked that "events are only the froth on things.... The
past as a precise idea has meaning and value only for the
man who is aware that he has a passion for the future."
Thus history has a plot for reading meaning and value into
mere events. In this sense all history is dramatic. C. B.
Purdom has argued that much tragedy is told from a retrospective point of view, for the course of events takes meaning from a vantage point requiring a backward vision, giving significance to episodes as if from foreknowledge,
regarding them from a future that endows them with
premonitions. Or, in Valéry's words, "The historian does
for the past what the fortune-teller does for the future. But
the fortuneteller takes the risk of being proved wrong, the
historian does not." He adds that history is "a magic book
in which we read nothing but what we think we ought to
be."

In genuine history, as distinct from mere chronicle, we
cannot detach the observer from what is observed, from the
"facts" he relates. The true historian, as distinct from the
mere chronologist, has his own view of the past. The
"scientific" 19th-century history was never truly "objective." As Valéry comments, "The past is an entirely mental
thing," conferring on history the power of novels and tales.
Collingwood bases his view of history on the same principle, for authentic history is a work of the imagination, like
a novel. "Factual" episodes are, for the historian, only
"paste and scissors" data that must be transformed by the
historian's reading of the past. True history penetrates the

"facts" with an interpretation that transvalues the past to an order of myth or, if you will, to an order of drama. The strawberry episode in *Richard III* remains as a deposit of mere chronicle, the uninterpreted past, the incident without context.

Norse documents like the *Landnamabok* or even the *Njala Saga* have the anecdotal temper of history-*manqué*. The bleak record of family feuds resembles, in its prosaic way, the genealogical chapters of the Old Testament, neutral summations in linear succession. In spite of their ironic understatement the sagas are more anecdotal than Thucydides' history of the Peloponnesian wars, for Thucydides imposes upon his chronicle a half-dramatic plot with its own implied judgment on Athenian policy. Thucydides's history has the moral meanings of Aeschylus's *The Persians*.

Chronicle, then, is narrative deprived of drama, a recitation without direction toward any imagined end. It is history in only one dimension, lacking preordained structure. This processional movement is often found in medieval art, as it is in the Bayeux tapestry. Dagobert Frey has defined the gothic mode of narrative as proceeding "from one item to the next" in an unfolding of time episode by episode, as if a film were rolled off in "continuous representation" but without any "synchronization of what is represented." The synchronization appeared in Renaissance painting, where the action is coordinated in all its relationships and proportions. Renaissance painting focuses the entire situation "simultaneously." But in medieval art, as Frey says, "Since the separate parts of the picture and the separate objects in the pictorial content are not seen simultaneously but successively, each element in the painting is independent, and fundamentally unrelated to others." In gothic narrative, the conception of space is conception of movement. Dante's *Commedia* is "directional," but unfolds in episodic linear time during his progress from Hell through Purgatory to Paradise.

That is to say, gothic art was a narrative extension, whereas Renaissance art was dramatic because it coordinated episodes into a more static vision, making time subordinate to spatial relationships. One can translate Frey's theory into Francis Fergusson's distinction between narrative and plot: the narrative is only the succession of events, but the plot is the dramatic "arrangement of incidents" in a form having closely reciprocal relations or reflexive reference. Plot (*mythos* in Aristotle's sense) is a synoptic vision of the entire action, bringing the episodes into simultaneous focus; in plot the events cohere in a static pattern or design, preordaining the meaning and scaling the incidents against each other as if one had foreknowledge of the outcome. If gothic art is a linear narrative, Renaissance art is a labyrinthine plan. Plot, as different from narrative, is a juxtaposition that is spatial as well as temporal, and is demonstrative, much as a Euclidean proposition being worked through is demonstrative. Aristotle's notion of plot requires a kind of retrospective view on the part of author, hero, and audience.

Something of this retrospective view distinguishes history from chronicle, since authentic history has its "plot" worked out by the historian. Collingwood considers true history to be a projection of present consciousness into past events, a reexperiencing of the past, a resurrection in the present of what is chronologically bygone. History is dramatic insofar as it is a reenacting, imaginatively, of occurrences that are inaccessible to present consciousness until memory transforms them into relived experiences. So history performs what Wordsworth asked of poetry: a reconstruction of the past, which by contemplation is recovered with increased meaning until it "does itself actually exist in the mind." This recovery of the experience is "kindred" to the original experience. Authentic history is "literature," unlike the annal, which fixates the past as remote and "done." Jacqueline de Romilly remarks that Greek tragedy was born with the new sense of history.

In the history plays Shakespeare imaginatively resurrects the past by reading into it certain moral judgments. Yet the movement in these plays is often "processional," much as the movement in the mystery plays and Dante's *Commedia* is processional or episodic, and there are passages of mere chronicle quite out of key with a dramatic vision of the past. One such passage in *Richard III* with this accelerated chronicle tempo is Gloucester's review of his machinations—a passage lacking the psychic dimension of true history:

> The son of Clarence have I pent up close,
> His daughter meanly have I matched in marriage,
> The sons of Edward sleep in Abraham's bosom,
> And Anne my wife hath bid this world good night. (IV, 3)

This hasty review has the pace not only of chronicle but of farce. Such passages are at odds with others that transcend chronicle and bring to the drama a consciousness that is not linear or successive but contemplative and, finally, moral.

The second time sense in *Richard III* is cyclic and is voiced in the choral judgment of old Queen Margaret, who speaks with more dramatic accent than chronicle allows:

> They that stand high have many blasts to shake them,
> And if they fall, they dash themselves to pieces. (I, 3)

Here is the voice heard in the very title of John Lydgate's *Falls of Princes*, echoed from Boccaccio's *De Casibus Virorum Illustrum*, proclaiming that by the rotation of Fortune's false wheel the mighty will be humbled. The cycle of Fortune is a chronometric pattern of human experience which medieval art inherited from the classics. It is represented everywhere in illustrations of the Wheel of Fortune: first as simply blind rotation, then, after Boethius, as an agency of divine governance. As Chaucer had it in "Le Pleintif Countre Fortune":

> This wrecched worldes transmutacioun,
> As wele or wo, now povre and now honour,

Withouten ordre or wys discretioun
Governed is by Fortunes errour.

The medieval idea of tragedy depended upon the rotation
of Fortune's wheel, the prologue to the Monk's Tale commenting:

Tragedie is to seyn a certeyn storie,
As olde bookes maken us memorie,
Of hym that stood in greet prosperitee,
And is yfallen out of heigh degree
Into myserie, and endeth wrecchedly.

The image of the mutability of Fortune, "now up, now
doun, as boket in a welle," is tinged with a moral implication that pride goes before a fall. This implication is found
in Sophocles, who was always reminding us that no man
can be counted happy until he is dead. Associated, too, is
the Greek dread of *hubris,* the *hyperbasia* or insolence of one
provoking the jealousy of gods who lop off the heads of the
mighty. The theme of humbling the proud is also Biblical,
as Job suggests, and probably arises from a primitive or
tribal sense that power is treacherous, that eminence provokes calamity. *Hubris* is not mentioned in Aristotle's discussion of tragedy, but is perhaps concealed behind his
view of the tragic figure as one who fails because of some
blindness or blunder, committing him to a disastrously
wrong choice.

In any case the tragedy of Fortune is basically cyclic, a
course of events that returns upon itself; and it may be
related to oriental notions of time as recurrent. According
to this primitive intuition of human events, time is not a
linear sequence but a closed circuit that repeats itself until
some millenium begins the world's great age anew. This
cyclic time sense assumes that there is nothing new in
history; it is radically different from the Christian (and
earlier Hebraic) eschatological view that history is moving
toward a destined end. Under the auspices of a grim fatality

of inevitable cycles, time becomes anguish or *douleia* from which we cannot escape, especially if we attain success.

The growth of Orphic, then Christian, yearning for redemption from time is testimony to ancient man's efforts to be released from endless revolutions of death and rebirth, which in turn must have been associated with the rituals of fertility cycles. Something of the rebellion against Fortune's cycles is heard in the Player's speech in *Hamlet*:

> Out, out, thou strumpet Fortune! All you gods,
> In general synod take away her power,
> Break all the spokes and fellies from her wheel,
> And bowl the round nave down the hill of heaven,
> As low as to the fiends. (II, 2)

Fortune as entirely blind and Fortune as the fall of the mighty: both appear in Shakespeare's plays. In *Henry V* Fluellen refers to Fortune as entirely indiscriminate:

> . . . Fortune is painted plind, with a muffler afore her eyes, to signify to you that Fortune is plind; and she is painted also with a wheel, to signify to you, which is the moral of it, that she is turning and inconstant, and mutability and variation; and her foot, look you, is fixed upon a spherical stone, which rolls, and rolls, and rolls. (III, 6)

Then there is the oracular voice of Queen Margaret passing her saturnine verdict on the Yorkists in *Richard III*:

> So now prosperity begins to mellow
> And drop into the rotten mouth of death. (IV, 4)

Margaret speaks like one who knows that the mighty are not mighty forever and that the whore Fortune eventually makes all men equal in adversity—for the cuckold Calamity is wedded to us all. Though the cycle of Fortune does not involve the fully tragic meaning that disaster is self-inflicted, it does give a dramatic value to the course of time and projects *Richard III* beyond the loose, inconsequential, and neutral progress of the chronicle.

Margaret's rotational time sense lurks everywhere behind plays like *Richard II* and the drama of the Lancastrians, who destroy him. Margaret brings Sophoclean overtones into Shakespearean history. The rotational action of
Fortune is also a force in that bleak play, *Timon of Athens*,
where the cyclic course of time is traced in the reverses that
bring down the wealthy—glittering gold here transposing
the medieval aristocratic view of Fortune into a new Renaissance context, the "quick blows of Fortune" struck in
the free and open market, as they are in *The Merchant of
Venice*. In *Timon* the Poet, speaking without the choral reso-
nance of Margaret's classic prophecy, observes:

> When Fortune in her shift and change of mood
> Spurns down her late beloved, all his dependants,
> Which labored after him to the mountain's top
> Even on their knees and hands, let him slip down,
> Not one accompanying his declining foot. (I, 1)

This sounds a little like *Lear* or, more prophetically, like
Balzac, and is harsh with the realism of an age of commercial enterprise. The "high and pleasant hill" on which
"feigned Fortune" is throned is no longer a regal eminence,
but one where "glib and slippery creatures" strive upward
like the mediocre characters in Balzac's *Human Comedy*.
Such creatures reappear in *Troilus and Cressida*, another
play committed to the ravages of Fortune.

But Margaret's speech on prosperity destined to drop
into the rotten mouth of death introduces a third conception of time—the primitive and deeply moral conviction
that time brings retribution for wrongs done. Margaret
speaks with a double voice, and her undertone is a primal
one, vibrant with the epic code of the *lex talionis*, the wrong
for wrong as it is heard in Aeschylus' *Oresteia*:

> . . . Say that right for right
> Hath dimmed your infant morn to aged night. (IV, 4)

This is Margaret's most impressive choral utterance, for she speaks of the penalty that must befall those who violate the moral law inherent in the cosmos.

This moral law of equity magnifies the local prescriptions of the tribe into universal commandments, the codes accepted by Greek and Hebrew in the ancient world. *Leviticus* and the *Iliad* are based upon such a code: blood must be atoned by blood, wrong by wrong. Here is the frightful law dictated by the Erynnes, and they presuppose a time scheme that is judicial and abiding. For the epic mind, all history is a manifestation or endorsement of these timeless laws, which imply a radically ethical sanction in nature.

Under the dispensation of these eternal laws tragedy is no longer simply the fall of the mighty, the temporal mutability of Fortune. Instead, it is an equation to be struck, balancing injury for injury in a distribution that insures parity. F. M. Cornford once pointed out that this ancient sense of the equity of fate, so important in tragedy, is spatial as well as temporal. Margaret phrases this epic equation when she says to the Yorkist Elizabeth:

> I had an Edward, till a Richard killed him;
> I had a Harry till a Richard killed him;
> Thou hadst an Edward till a Richard killed him;
> Thou hadst a Richard till a Richard killed him . . .
> O upright, just, and true-disposing God,
> How do I thank thee that this carnal cur
> Preys on the issue of his mother's body. . . . (IV, 4)

As if instinctively, Shakespeare has phrased the equation in balanced staves.

Just as Margaret shifts from the theme of Fortune's cycle to the theme of wrong-for-wrong so Aeschylus in the *Agamemnon* shifts from the old idea that the gods strike down the mighty to the view of fate as retribution. First there is the primal fear of success, for the black furies stalk the fortunate man and drop him into darkness. Then this theme of mutability changes into a moral equation: the evil act breeds others. The chorus chants:

> Here is anger for anger . . .
> The spoiler is robbed; he killed; he has paid.
> The truth stands ever beside God's throne
> Eternal: he who has wrought shall pay; that is the law.

The beam balances by a tragic law of justice when Right exacts atonement:

> . . . blood stroke for blood
> Shall be paid . . . So speaks
> The voice of age-old wisdom.

Finally, in *Eumenides* the epic equation of strength colliding with strength, wrong with wrong, changes to another theme of atonement under political law, making possible a purgation that strikes an equation by suffering.

Thus Aeschylus voices two contradictory interpretations of time that recur in *Richard III*, namely, the law that "they that stand high have many blasts to shake them," and the law that "Wrong hath but wrong, and blame the due of blame." Behind the first law lies the temporal insecurity of man's achievement and the feeling that the gods delight in reducing the eminent. Behind the second is a more ethical principle that the cosmos is ordered by some canon of justice. (Either law implies that man learns by suffering.) Like the voice of retribution, Margaret stands behind the other characters as if she were casting roles they must play to fit an epic equation:

> Thus hath the course of justice whirled about
> And left thee but a very prey to time. (IV, 4)

This sense of time as an agent of justice is tinged with a primitive social intuition that every man must have his equitable share or *moira*, his due portion of the spoils or the land, the property that, in the Old Testament phrase, is divided by lot.

These views of time as mere chronological procession of events, as cyclic Fortune, or as retribution are related to Heidegger's distinction between the *Mitwelt* and the *Umwelt*—each world having its own kind of time. The *Umwelt* is the realm of our experience in the physical world of things and of happenings occurring in chronometric time. It is the world of annal and chronicle, the record of successive events. But the *Mitwelt* is a world where we live with others, a social world of shared experience, a world with derived human meaning where equity is represented either by the rotations of Fortune or by some canon of justice, distribution, or retribution.

In the *Mitwelt* time is not simple chronology but a sign of group relations: the mighty eventually fall, sin is visited by penalty, or some just dispensation is expected. The *Mitwelt* is a domain of moral import. It is a world of civil time, whether in the political order of due succession to kingship, insuring legitimacy and stability, or in the generational hierarchy of youth and age, as in *Lear*. In *Hamlet*, in *Macbeth*, in *Troilus and Cressida*, in the Henry plays there are canons of degree, priority, and place, for civil time requires a "line of order" that must not be disrupted. The Elizabethans had a nearly epic sense of civil time, which seemed to them an aspect of the great chain of being. The course of justice to which Margaret refers is a law of the *Mitwelt*, depending not upon any arbitrary will of the gods but on a rubric of social being; not upon a cycle of mutability alone but on a need to regulate the exercise of power, privilege, or authority.

F. M. Cornford called this canon the provincial ordering of the world, an elemental social *logos* apportioning to each his *moira*. This local law of sharing is projected, on a larger scale, into the dominion of nature. It is a law older than the Olympian gods. The intimation that each man during his

life will be meted out his share is felt in Aeschylus and
Sophocles, even if Sophocles has some anxiety that man is
victimized by the insecurity of time, *Chronos*. In Euripides,
as in Shakespeare's *Troilus and Cressida*, the notion of justice
seems to break down, and man is left facing only Chance
or *Tyche*, which strikes no intelligible equations. This disillusion, so closely associated with the view of Mutability as
irrational, is phrased in *Troilus and Cressida* by Agamemnon, a Euripidean character who makes a mockery of time
as justice:

> The ample proposition that hope makes
> In all designs begun on earth below
> Fails in the promised largeness. (I, 3)

So there is left only the ruin of purpose, desire, valor. As
Agamemnon puts it:

> What's past and what's to come is strewed with husks
> And formless ruin of oblivion. (IV, 5)

Always behind *Richard III*, however, there is the nearly
epic and half-spatial notion of the balance that justice
finally insures during the course of time. The play is almost
Greek in its sense of the madness of crime, the mania
known in the *Iliad* as *Ate*, the seizure that robs man of
sanity. And just as certain families live under a curse *(Ara)*,
so Richard is constantly identified as a monster, a bunch-
back toad, a rooting abortive hog, an abnormality in nature.
This creature must be expelled from English history, for he
is a thing of Caliban darkness casting his shadow over his
family. If Clytemnestra is a man-souled woman, an abomi-
nation, Richard is a boar let loose to wreak havoc wherever
he comes.

Yet Richard does not finally disrupt the provincial ordering of a world ruled by the ethic that epic transmitted to
tragedy. When death overtakes him at Bosworth Field, he
recognizes with almost Sophoclean fatalism "All un-

avoided is the doom of destiny." Buckingham is a mere
agent for Richard's crimes, and yet he, too, goes to the block
speaking like some personage in Sophocles:

> That high All-seer which I dallied with
> Hath turned my feigned prayer on my head
> And given in earnest what I begged in jest.
> Thus doth He force the swords of wicked men
> To turn their own points in their masters' bosoms.
> Thus Margaret's curse falls heavy on my neck . . .
> Wrong hath but wrong, and blame the due of blame. (V, 1)

This is the irony of classic tragedy, unlike the irony in
medieval stories with their merely temporal change of Fortune. Classic irony is an irony of justice, not of time alone;
it allots us the share so inevitably ours as ordained by our
nature and our choice. It is an irony of ignorance apparent
in Oedipus, who finds that when he had eyes he did not see.
It is the irony of *Othello*.

It is an irony arising from a recognition of guilt and
belongs to the third world in which we live: the *Eigenwelt*.[4]
In contrast to our consciousness in the *Umwelt* and the
Mitwelt, the *Eigenwelt* is the arena of our private recognitions known most intimately when the self, facing the self,
identifies one's being in an experience not shared by others.
It is a world where chronology is irrelevant; we simply
reach an awareness of our nature, knowing what we have
been, are, and will be. In the *Eigenwelt* we cross the boundary from social consciousness to the consciousness of selfhood—the self regarding the self in a psychic drama with
its own *anagnorisis*. Our sins may be social, an offense
against an accepted code, but our guilt is ours alone, a
personal appropriation of our sense of wrongdoing.

Thus the law of retribution works itself out in two different spheres of experience, the social and the private, sin and
guilt. The epic is primarily devoted to the social canon of
retribution, as we see in the *Iliad*, where Achilles is de-

prived of his share by Agamemnon and behaves badly by sulking in his tent, leaving the Greeks to suffer at the hands of the Trojans. Achilles sins by sending Patroklos to fight. Then Patroklos's death prompts his sense of guilt, causing a change in his nature, and makes him dimly see himself for what he is. Sin is transgression against the tribe; guilt is the inward burden of self-judgment borne in the *Eigenwelt.* One can sin, especially in the epic, without feeling guilt.

Achilles' resentment is grounded in the sense that he has been disgraced publicly when Agamemnon takes Briseis. He loses "face," an injury that must be retributed, and is retributed when Agamemnon returns more than the "share" he has taken. This epic retribution is consistent with the "shame culture" of primitive groups. But Achilles passes over the margin from "shame culture" to "guilt culture" (that is, tragic culture) when he realizes that he is personally accountable, in his blindness and wrath, for the death of his friend; and his guilt becomes a form of self-recognition. This self-recognition takes place in the privacy of the *Eigenwelt,* at a new height of consciousness.

Richard III, like the *Iliad,* hovers between the *Mitwelt* and the *Eigenwelt,* pointing toward the self-awareness of Macbeth without, however, reaching the full tragic experience of a personal appropriation of guilt. The action in *Richard III* occurs mostly in the *Mitwelt;* it is a play filled with sin, with only a few moments of guilt when conscience prevails.

But these few moments of guilt project the drama into a fourth time-scheme, supplementing the other time schemes of chronicle, fortune, and epic retribution. For a few instants there stirs within Richard the private and timeless consciousness of guilt, a recognition of what he has been, is, and will be. During the night before Bosworth Field, while Richard lies wakeful, he is disturbed by the nightmare vision of those he has murdered, who return from his past to vex his present in the kind of anachronism we find in *Macbeth*. Afflicted momentarily by self-judgment, Richard foreshadows Macbeth's anguish of self-identification:

> Richard loves Richard: that is, I am I.
> Is there a murderer here? No. Yes, I am;
> Then fly. What, from myself? Great reason why—
> Lest I revenge. What, myself upon myself?
> Alack, I love myself. . . .
> O no, alas I rather hate myself
> For hateful deeds committed by myself.
> I am a villain— yet I lie, I am not.
> Fool, of thyself speak well. Fool, do not flatter.
> My conscience hath a thousand several tongues,
> And every tongue brings in a several tale
> And every tale condemns me for a villain. . . .
> All several sins, all used in each degree,
> Throng to the bar, crying all, "Guilty! Guilty!" (V, 3)

Alone in his *Eigenwelt,* Richard has an apprehension that occurs in psychic, not chronological, time, the time that anachronistically fuses past, present, and future in an intense recognition of his abiding nature. The conscience is oracular, and in a more waking instant Richard refers to this anachronism when he exclaims in despair, like Macbeth:

> . . . I am in
> So far in blood that sin will pluck on sin,
> Tear-falling pity dwells not in this eye. (IV, 2)

Richard is reported by his wife Anne to have had such moments of foreknowledge in his dreams:

> For never yet one hour in his bed
> Did I enjoy the golden dew of sleep
> But with his timorous dreams was still awaked. (IV, 1)

This tragic self-appraisal is an assumption of responsibility for one's nature, a consciousness that makes the course of time and the changes in Fortune secondary to a vision

of self. Since one is what one was and will be, all notions
of character "development" are extraneous. In a tragic
view of the self, with its ironic recognitions, there is only
a disclosure that character is fate—in one's beginning is
one's end. Richard's perception of the anachronism in his
fate resembles Macbeth's identification of himself in a terrible moment of introspection showing that his future is at
one with his past. By this synoptic understanding of his
past, present, and future, Macbeth, like Richard, passes a
ruthless self-judgment, the self-judgment that brings
Othello to see, like Oedipus, that he was always blind.

In his book on *Greek Tragedy,* H. D. F. Kitto makes a
distinction between a tragic figure and a tragic character.
The tragic figure performs theatrical gestures without necessarily exhibiting tragic consciousness. Aeschylus' Agamemnon is "doomed from the start," yet lacks the self-
awareness, the inward dimension of a tragic character like
Oedipus. If Agamemnon is a tragic figure, Macbeth, like
Oedipus, has a height of consciousness that brings self-
recognition. Richard III is a tragic figure who has moments
when he becomes a tragic character. So far as theatrical
action goes, Richard has every chance to establish tragic
consciousness; but the play is largely given to gestures and
rhetoric without fully exploiting the self-appraisal that torments Macbeth. The accelerated tempo of the play—its
chronometric rapidity—militates against the slow tragic
pace which depends not on theatrical activity but on the
tidal flow of psychic life.

Othello competes with *Richard III* in the barbarity of its
action, but it pauses amid the perplexities of tragic consciousness, the dilemmas of a tragic character who in debate with himself retards the theatrical movement to give
monumental breadth to the realization. The Oedipus experience is deliberate and retarded in the same way, having
the demonstrative quality of a proof after which one can
write Q.E.D. The so-called action in *Oedipus* or *Othello* is a

penetration of the labyrinth inside which the tragic character finds himself at the overwhelming moment when he
discerns his nature: there never was an escape, though he
can see why and how he is inside. This order of drama is
a recognition of what one is rather than an action unfolding
in narrative sequence.

Full tragic consciousness requires a certain suspension of
chronology, an intuition of the present in relation to past
and future. The tragic recognition or *anagnorisis* is like an
arrest of time. It presents time as *lived*—existential time.
The time of annal or chronicle is dead time, alien time,
irrecoverable time, time seen as a neutral record—time of
which neither history nor tragedy can be made, for it is not
endured. The bygone, irrecoverable time of the annal is
chronology untouched by poetry—linear, progressive, one-
dimensional, and sometimes directionless. The time of Fortune's wheel is closed—linear, but returning upon itself in
cycles. The time of retribution—the tribal equation or the
provincial ordering of the world—is also in a sense closed
time, for the future is determined by the balance that must
be struck between deeds.

The spatial logic of equations that must be struck determines the course of a play like Aeschylus's *Suppliants,*
where the law of sanctuary exacts a kind of piety: Pelasgus
must not deny refuge to the daughters of Danaus lest he
violate the code that will bring retribution on him and on
his people. Even if the choice is hard and the future is dark,
he must open his gates to the maidens seeking shelter. To
refuse refuge would be a sin. There is no problem of personal guilt, however. The Greeks shared with the ancient
Hebrews this tribal ethic of retribution—breaking the law
is sin, and the sin is visited upon the sinner.

The Greeks supplemented the law of retribution for sin
by a quite private or personal sense of guilt, a sense that
arose in Greek culture when Athenian humanism achieved
an awareness of the identity of the self. The onset of this

sense of selfhood and individual responsibility led to the
form of drama we call tragedy. Aeschylus's *Seven Against
Thebes* deals with sin, but without any sense of guilt. Sophocles' *Philoctetes* is a play dealing not with sin but with guilt
—the urgent need in Neoptolemus to be honest in his own
eyes. The transition between the old, half-epic drama and
the new drama of guilt is made during the course of Aeschylus's *Oresteia,* where the sins of the House of Atreus are
finally purged through Orestes' redemption from his guilt.

Richard III almost conjugates the stages by which drama
passes from old tribal sin to the more civilized and humane
recognition of guilt. The play looks backward to the chronicle and forward to mature tragedy. In Richard's solilo-
quies there appears not only a lively half-comic, half-
pathetic consciousness of his abnormality but also an
awareness of his outrageous delinquencies, thus drawing
the focus centripetally toward a recognition of his own
responsibility for his situation. This vision of the self is an
infinite moment. It is a recognition that requires an imagination lacking in the tribal or epic code. *Richard III* with its
inconsistent time schemes charts the emergence of tragic
time from the time of chronicle and epic.

II
Political Time:
The Vanity of History

Richard III is a "history" play, but hardly in the sense that the tetralogy of *Richard II, Henry IV: Parts I* and *II,* and *Henry V* are "history" plays, for the latter deal with politics as *Richard III* does not. That is, the tetralogy revolves about the modern issues of power, whereas the malignity of Richard III seems like a grotesque theatrical interlude. *Richard III* is a caricature of politics; the Henry plays are *Realpolitik,* dealing with history as we have lately lived it. They have, for us, a disturbing authenticity. The criminal career of Richard III involved no policies; the Henry plays are studies in Lancastrian policy. Shakespeare understands the political games we have been playing since the Renaissance, questioning the relation of power to morality.

However he may overextend his case. Jan Kott shrewdly states that the Henry plays treat power as "something abstract and mythological, almost a pure idea," a "grand mechanism" to penalize the weak, making them guilty. This exercise of power was in turn a reflex of the new freedom of the will studied in Machiavelli's *Prince.*

Machiavelli secularized politics, and his premises are phrased at the opening of his book: "The wish to acquire is in truth very natural and common, and men always do so when they can, and for this they will be praised, not blamed." Such endorsement of power brings into the foreground of history an impulse as old as the epic. But in the epic power was placed in the social context of a code of equity, sharing, and measure. In epic and epical drama, as in the voice of old Queen Margaret in *Richard III*, power was qualified by the piety of an ancient law of retribution, a postulate of the provincial ordering of the world.

In Machiavelli the piety vanishes. In fact, piety itself is an instrument useful in politics. The Prince is left to make his own way, and Machiavelli asks whether regents "have to use prayers or can they use force?" If they use prayer, "they always succeed badly, and never compass anything; but when they can rely on themselves and use force, then they are rarely endangered." So the successful Prince will employ "all those injuries which it is necessary for him to inflict," and will rely on arms, which must be the foundation of good law. Nor need he dread the reproach of cruelty, since "it is much safer to be feared than loved." The Prince must learn to be a beast as well as a man, both lion and fox. A policy of power will exempt him from the cycle of Fortune at least to a degree, for "fortune is the arbiter of one half of our actions, but she still leaves us to direct the other half, or perhaps a little less."

There was great malaise about this creed, as there was when Athens long ago used it with entire self-awareness in subjecting the little island of Melos. Thucydides reports, in dramatic form, the brutal honesty of the Athenians, who assured the helpless Melians:

> Of the gods we believe, and of men we know, that by a necessary law of their nature they rule wherever they can . . . ; all we do is to make use of it, knowing that you and everybody else, having the same power as we have, would do the same as we do. Thus, as far as the gods are concerned, we have no fear and no reason to fear that we shall be at a disadvantage.

Euripides' plays are filled with repercussions from this episode; so too *Troilus and Cressida* is a Shakespearean repercussion from Machiavellian politics. During the debate about keeping Helen, Hector's great speech, derived from Aristotelian ethic, is a rebuttal of the principles of power politics. Hector pleads with the Trojans for a "free determination 'twixt right and wrong," arguing that if Helen be the wife of Menelaus, the "moral laws of nature and of nations" prescribe that she be returned to the Greeks. Hector's speech is like a footnote to Erasmus or Grotius.

So the Renaissance was hard put to deny the validity of Machiavelli's politics, which by exercise of the Prince's will suspended not only moral codes but, at least partially, the cycle of Fortune. The "moral laws of nature and of nations" having been sadly shaken, the Renaissance needed to counter Machiavellian policy by some alternative principles. Thus it resorted to certain anti-Machiavellian theses, none of which proved very effectual, as Shakespeare's plays indicate. Among these anti-Machiavellian theses were: the already outworn doctrine of the divinity hedging a king, the ideal of honor in the prince, the associated idea that the prince must be a creditable man, and the equivocal notion of redeeming the time.

Shakespeare deals with all these themes, but his distinctive anti-Machiavellian reaction is his new and very sensitive response to the past arising partly from a reinterpretation of the rotation of Fortune's wheel and partly from an intensely dramatic perception that the course of history has been nothing but a masquerade. Shakespeare's sense that this masquerade—this empty pageant of power—has been a blood bath heightens the pathos of the past, giving it existential value. Often in Shakespeare history seems like a triviality or mere tableau where political expediencies are seen against the vast backward and abysm of time. For Shakespeare has the new Renaissance consciousness of the infinite, the opening of illimitable distances like the blue

backgrounds in paintings by Leonardo or Patinir or Herri
Met de Bles, like a world dissolved, like Prospero's vision-
ary horizon against which we are transient dreamwork.
For Shakespeare history can seem to be one more illusion.
This is his dramatic reply to Machiavelli, who lacked po-
etry.

Power and pathos in history, the divinity and honor of
the prince, the need to redeem the time—the Henry tetralogy is like an analysis of such themes in Renaissance
politics, each ambiguous as if Shakespeare could not find
his way to a convincing resolution. Within these plays are
the radically inconsistent premises of the Elizabethan mentality of crisis. However they were affected by a medieval
tendency to read history as a homily, the plays anticipate
the final secularization of politics that causes Nietzsche to
proclaim, "The gods are dead; let the superman be born."
The political crisis extends beyond the history plays, for
Claudius, Fortinbras, Macbeth, Antony, and Lear's daughters are all involved in the grand strategy of power strug-
gles.

In the Henry plays history is a new kind of chronicle
examining codes of political strategy. Shakespeare resisted
this merely strategic reading of history, but not with entire
success, or at least not without some confusion. He seems
never to have found an entirely satisfactory context for the
use of power; but he attempted what Machiavelli did not
attempt: to find such a context. As Northrop Frye has said,
"In Shakespeare there are, in practice, certain moral limits
to leadership." Shakespeare's problem is ours—to provide
some moral context for using the ever more terrifying
power at our disposal.

The Henry tetralogy is a continuing exploration of alternatives, each bringing its own dilemma. Many have discussed how Shakespeare, unable to regard history as naked
power politics, is indebted to the morality play with its
emphasis upon the penalties for the king's misconduct, or,

on the other hand, for regicide. Shakespeare was much occupied with the nature of the ideal king, always placing Machiavellian policy in an unMachiavellian context, hesitating to endorse a wholly secular meaning to history.

In the background of the tetralogy is the figure of Richard II, a symbol of the divinity hedging the king. Old Carlisle, hearing how Bolingbroke will seize Richard's crown, protests that no subject can sentence his sovereign. With the same choral voice we hear in Queen Margaret, Carlisle predicts that if Bolingbroke is crowned the blood of English will soak the ground and future ages will groan for this foul act. The course of the plays confirms the truth of Carlisle's foreboding, and yet Shakespeare is unable fully to confirm the divine right of kings, for the figure of Glendower is a parody of the royal image of Richard, suggesting the fraudulence of the claim that the king is God's vicegerent, above the jurisdiction of men. Glendower is, in fact, the *reductio ad absurdum* of the divinity of kings when he claims that at his nativity:

> The front of heaven was full of fiery shapes
> Of burning cressets, and at my birth
> The frame and huge foundation of the earth
> Shaked like a coward. (*Henry IV: Part I,* III, 1)

With sane and secular realism, Hotspur replies, "Why so it would have done at the same season if your mother's cat had but kittened."

So Shakespeare is thrown back on his other theme regarding royalty, that the good king must be a good man—a theme that, again, is a critique of the Machiavellian image of the Prince as lion and fox. By both criteria Richard II fails entirely; he not only thieves but verifies the Machiavellian truism that the king must be strong enough to use the power that endows him. Richard is a weakling filled with self-pity, and his pathos cannot exempt him from the penalty of failure:

> What must the king do now? Must he submit?
> The king shall do it. Must he be deposed?
> The king shall be contented. Must he lose
> The name of king? A God's name, let it go! (III, 3)

England needs Bolingbroke, who by Machiavellian principles justly sends Richard to his obscure little grave.

Woven in with Richard's failure is the old resignation to
the cycle of Fortune's wheel. Deposed Richard, extending
his crown to Henry IV, brings in the theme (which is
repeated when Bolingbroke himself faces Hal in the Jerusalem chamber):

> Now is this golden crown like a deep well
> That owes two buckets, filling one another,
> The emptier ever dancing in the air,
> The other down, unseen, and full of water.
> That bucket down and full of tears am I,
> Drinking my griefs whilst you mount up on high. (IV, 1)

Associated too with this Chaucerian alternation is the
lyrical melancholy pervading the entire tetralogy, suggesting that the king is but a man after all. Machiavelli had
introduced into politics the schizoid notion that a bad man
could be a good prince, or conversely, a good man could be
a bad prince. Consequently there appears the disrelationship between public and private character, leading to the
depersonalizing of politics, making it a form of role-playing. For in such politics the mask is more real than the face;
the Prince must drop his face to exhibit his mask. The act
is more real than the actor. Or is it? As a dramatist, Shakespeare continually raised doubts about the validity of role-
playing. He was ever inclined to distrust the very theatrical
medium in which he worked, and his plays are filled with
references to the deceptive nature of dramatic representation. In the Henry tetralogy he is almost obsessively concerned with the relation between the nature of the king as
man and the role he played as king. In this way Shakespeare's reading of history is radically dramatic.

The relation between the man and the king—here is an aspect of Renaissance humanism. As Richard sits upon the ground speaking of graves and epitaphs, he recognizes that the king is as vulnerable to calamity and death as his meanest subjects. Like them he feeds on bread, tastes grief, and meets the disasters from which his royal role cannot protect him. In such passages—and in the great scene between Hal and his father in the Jerusalem chamber—Shakespeare has a perception Machiavelli never attained, namely, that the play of political power is only another imposture enacted in time. As Richard says, "nothing can we call our own but death,"

> And that small model of the barren earth
> Which serves as paste and cover to our bones. (III, 2)

The antic death, sitting within the hollow crown, keeps court among kings, mocking at pomp and allowing the Prince to monarchize with "self and vain conceit" until at a prick the whole empty pageant ceases. Machiavelli lacked this pathos of time, this longer and more human perspective on politics.

Having acknowledged the defenceless humanity of kings, Shakespeare is led to that other anti-Machiavellian thesis at the heart of the history plays, the theme of honor, through which Machiavelli finessed his way with specious ease. Though Shakespeare is fully aware of the validity or the necessity of honor, this value in history is frequently uncertain and often deceptive, the mere scutcheon Falstaff finds it. Noble and appealing as the ideal of honor may be, Shakespeare does not rely upon it as an assured moral principle operative in history. Behind, or within, the ideal of the king's honor always lurks the implication that, as Lenin put it, in politics there is no morality, only expediency. There is enough cynicism in the Henry plays to indicate how deeply Shakespeare was affected by the wound Machiavelli gave modern politics.

In Hal, the most attractive of the Lancastrians, honor

could be said to replace the ideal of the divinity of kings.
And yet Hal himself tarnished the ideal of honor by stroke
after stroke of effective strategy, especially in the outrageous imperialism of his incursion into France. The Lancastrian line never allowed honor to inhibit the realism of
their policy. Falstaff has the privilege of deflating this
hypertrophied value: if he that died Wednesday for some
airy notion has honor, then honor is only a word. Besides,
it is not Hal, but Hotspur, who embodies the unqualified
principle of honor—Hotspur, with his romantic wrong-
headedness and passion, voices the ideal of honor and the
foolish honesty that the Prince may have. But the leap to
pluck bright honor from the moon is not so easy as Hotspur
supposed, and it is an insane venture anyhow, as Hamlet
knew when he meditated on that other sweet prince, Fortinbras, who embarked on an enterprise as headlong as
Hotspur's, finding quarrel in a straw, fighting for a plot
that could not hold the slain. Honor as an ultimate value
seems to be a variety of neurosis, a compulsion that is
politically rash, a perversion of the use of power.

So over against the outworn faith in the divinity of kings,
the secular ideal of honor is hardly tenable as a strategic
principle. To this degree Shakespeare subscribes to Machiavelli. Yet the need for honor rings like a refrain
through Shakespeare's plays, heard in Antony's dealings
with Caesar and in Pompey's refusal to cut the throats of
his competitors when they feast as his guests. It is symptomatic, however, that honor is cherished most by the losers
in history. Shakespeare seems forced back to a qualified
Machiavellian policy that should be used by a king who is
also a responsible man. Here we are on the most ambiguous
ground of all, for this ideal requires a Prince who is able
to temporize by adapting the ethic of honor to pragmatic
or utilitarian policy.

Henry IV, having liquidated Richard for the good of
England as well as in his own interest, rejects the very

poison he found it prudent to use, saying that his soul is full of woe because of the blood he thought it expedient to shed. The murderer puts on the mask of the moralist. Then Hal, descending into Eastcheap, plays the same equivocal game at the bohemian plane:

> I know you all, and will awhile uphold
> The unyoked humor of your idleness. (I, 2)

Hal's father confesses that he himself used much the same tactic while Richard ambled with shallow jesters; Henry seemed the nobler when he found the moment to ascend. The Lancastrians are able to exploit the time, establishing themselves by an opportunism that is Machiavellian. They are salutary Machiavellians. One of the most comprehending appraisals of political power is Henry's comment, "Are these things then necessities? Then let us meet them like necessities."

The Lancastrians are creatures of time who can manipulate the occasion. By contrast, Falstaff is a creature who is timeless. Born late in the day, he is an archetypal figure exempt from the casualties of history until Hal rejects him. At the start of *Henry IV,* when Falstaff asks, "What time of day is it, lad?," Hal replies almost symbolically, "What a devil hast thou to do with the time of the day?"—a "superfluous" query on Falstaff's part. If the Lancastrians are strategic, Falstaff is instinctual. Falstaff is able to respond biologically, so that when he is caught lying about the robbery at Gadshill, he claims that he was "a coward on instinct," for "instinct is a great matter."

Falstaff brings into history an animal faculty for survival by an adaptability that was not scientifically defined until the 19th century. He is a natural being like Nietzsche's satyr creatures existing behind the facade of history, and he dies at the ebbing of the tide. In his greatest biological speech after the battle of Shrewsbury, Falstaff identifies his timeless instinctual existence by affirming that he is no counterfeit figure in history but, like Christ himself, an embodiment of the perpetual vitality not to be quenched:

> To die is to be a counterfeit, for he is but the counterfeit of a man who hath not the life of a man; but to counterfeit dying when a man thereby liveth, is to be no counterfeit, but the true and perfect image of life indeed. (V, 4)

Falstaff's role-playing is unlike the role-playing of the Lancastrians since it springs from a primal *élan vital*, organically, not from preconceived policy. He is able to transform the Darwinian to the Dionysiac values. Falstaff responds tropistically; his mutations have an *ad hoc* rapidity, like the changing colors of the chameleon. His adaptability is not an act calculated in advance but an ecological reaction.

Only when he begins to play the Lancastrian game with Shallow does Falstaff fall victim to history and time. Until then he maintains himself as an image of Whitman's urge, procreant urge, the organic principle of life itself enduring beyond and behind political history to which he at last succumbs. By his descent into Eastcheap Hal participates in Falstaff's celebration of vitality.

Yet Hal belongs to political history, and the Lancastrians move through these plays with a double time sense: the sense, first, that they have a vocation, by using their political strategy, to redeem the time by a secular, half-Machiavellian policy; and secondly, by their sense that the very political history they create is only an insubstantial pageant in which they are transient actors. They sense that they can, and must, make history, but that history is a triviality when seen against the illimitable horizon of time.

Hal has this double, ironic vision even while he is in Eastcheap. "Well, thus we play the fools with the time," he says, "and the spirits of the wise sit in the clouds and mock us." Hotspur, too, at the moment of his death, has the same sardonic sense of the vanity of history:

> But thoughts, the slaves of life, and life time's fool,
> And time that takes survey of all the world
> Must have a stop. (V, 4)

Richard II likewise has this sense that the life of a king is an absurd charade; deposed by Bolingbroke, he is suddenly time's fool:

> . . . I am unkinged by Bolingbroke,
> And straight am nothing. But whate'er I be,
> Nor I nor any man that but man is,
> With nothing shall be pleased till he be eased
> With being nothing. (V, 5)

One of the touching moments in these plays comes when Henry IV, who has mastered history by dethroning Richard, lies awake saddened by the disorders in his kingdom, and meditates on the unfathomable reaches of time against which the course of history seems negligible. It may be the longest vision of time in Shakespeare, longer even than Macbeth's despairing vision of interminable yesterdays and tomorrows. The full and astonishing range of Henry's vision backward over time can be suggested by a model one of our scientists has devised to scale the age of the earth against man's history.[1] If we contract terrestrial time into the scale of a single calendar year, and the world began on January 1st, then life would not appear until early August. By October there would be the oldest fossils, by December reptilian life would have developed; mammals would evolve about Christmas, and on New Year's Eve, by five minutes to midnight, man would present himself. Recorded human history would occur in the interval while midnight strikes.

This reductive backward view is phrased in Henry's meditation, which is filled with the pathos of a time sense that only modern man could have, and which makes Machiavellian tactics seem like a jest:

O God! that one might read the book of fate,
And see the revolution of the times
Make mountains level, and the continent,
Weary of solid firmness, melt itself
Into the sea! And other times to see
The beachy girdle of the ocean
Too wide for Neptune's hips . . .
            . . . O, if this were seen,
The happiest youth, viewing his progress through,
What perils past, what crosses to ensue,
Would shut the book, and sit him down and die. (III, 1)

The passage has none of the cynicism of Macbeth's bitter speech, but springs from an awareness of fatality brought by the Renaissance time scale, the blue distance that was like an elegiac background to the intrigues of the Machiavellian Prince who makes himself master of fortune and his hour. Henry's nocturnal soliloquy gives the largest possible meaning to the Renaissance landscape-with-figures—that marvelously new art form, a feat of the Renaissance imagination where the image of man is seen against a cosmic, timeless projection, into which he is absorbed with a nearly Oriental intuition of totality. The only kind of surrender known to the Lancastrians comes in the guise of this new temporal consciousness, this receding horizon that obliterates history.

For Falstaff, too, history is only an interlude that confers the delusory value known as honor. At a remarkable moment in the Jerusalem chamber while Henry IV lies at point of death, he is able to take, at last, a Falstaffian view of political history. Henry admits to Hal that his whole career in historical time has been like an ephemeral role, and with a sadness that is like a counterpoint to Falstaff's cynical appraisal of honor, the dying Henry confesses to his son that God alone knows by what devious paths he got the crown:

For all my reign hath been but as a scene
Acting that argument. (IV, 5)

History is not only guilt; it is a mumming. At this moment Henry has a dramatic vision lacking in Machiavelli when he recommends the politics of success. Only the lengthened perspective of seeing history against the abyss of time could give this modern feeling of the vanity and pathos of politics, a pathos and comedy Machiavelli would not understand.

But this is only an episode in the Henry plays, and Hal, like his father, like his brother John, must play the game of politics to redeem the time. In his attempt to console Henry for the dereliction of Hal, Warwick predicts that Hal will

> . . . in the perfectness of time
> Cast off his followers, and their memory
> Shall as a pattern or a measure live,
> By which his grace must mete the lives of others,
> Turning past evils to advantages. (IV, 4)

For Hal as an agent in political history will manipulate morality itself and continue to play the game that his father played as opportunist. Hal must redeem the time by living in a time quite different from Falstaff's time; he must reject the ahistoric time of revelry, the changeless time of the saturnalia, and take his place in the foreground of Machiavellian strategic time. So also Prince John proves at Gaultree that he is the legitimate son of his father by the strategy of redressing the grievances of the rebellious nobles while he condemns them to death.

After his father has gone wild into his grave, Hal continues to play the historical game even more effectively than the elder Henry. Hal puts on the mask of responsibility and justice to legitimize his policy. Before invading France, he is at pains to certify by Salic law that he can with right and conscience claim the French crown. The appearance of legality gives this imperialist enterprise a color of righteousness. Falstaff is dead, but there was perhaps more integrity in his cynicism about honor than in Hal's barbaric threat to the citizens of Harfleur: if he attacks again, he will bury the city in ashes, and his soldiers with the license of bloody hands will mow down virgins and infants.

Hal at least partially redeems himself from the amorality of history the night before Agincourt when, being catechized by Williams the common foot soldier, he is compelled to examine the justice of his cause and to decide whether it is honorable. Hal's conviction that honor must be grounded in an accountable use of royal power—meaning, in effect, that the king must answer for the ills befalling his people—is a response to Richard II, to Hotspur, to Falstaff (and to Fortinbras). Thus morality is linked with history. Honor does not accrue from victory, but from the character of the regent who leads his people to victory, or to defeat. So the king must be one with his subjects, among the happy few who share the making of history.

Hal resolves his "identity crisis" as Hamlet could not— in the course of history itself. If Hamlet's "identity crisis" is resolved at all, it is resolved for Hamlet alone. Hal's case is otherwise; he finds himself in his commitment to his followers, in what Buber would term an I-Thou relation. Hal's freedom is not found in Eastcheap, for while he was in bohemia he had only freedom from his father's empty respectability. Hal's freedom is found at Agincourt, where there is not freedom *from* but freedom *to*.

Freedom means freedom to act. The Hamlet paralysis is gone, for Hamlet's quest for freedom *from* was partly responsible for his frustrations. Hamlet could not redeem the time, although at last he was able to redeem himself. Throughout the Henry plays and throughout *Hamlet* there is a counterpoint of the private and the public. Hamlet never moves outside the dilemmas of the private; thus he is not a sweet prince except by promise—never by political action. This is what links Hamlet with Richard II, who as a public figure is disastrous. Richard as a private figure, with his Hamlet-like self-indulgent sensibility, has a certain pathos, a large degree of humanity. Yet Richard's very consciousness of his frailty is self-regarding, much like Hamlet's consciousness of his sullied flesh, his nameless offenses. Hal is never self-indulgent to this extent, for Hal was able to command his roles as Hamlet and Richard are not. Hamlet and Richard are seduced by the roles they allow themselves to play. But from the first Hal—who has his own dramatic imagination—knows them all and is able to calculate the instant when one mask is to be dropped, and another put on.

Richard and Hamlet exist in the realm of the *Eigenwelt*. Hal realizes himself in the time of the *Mitwelt* and *Umwelt*. Hamlet and Richard could not play the game of history. Hal plays this game to the hilt, existing as a public figure. Further, insofar as time is subjective for Richard and Hamlet, it is a form of melancholia in Richard and a form of compulsion in Hamlet. For Hamlet the times are out of joint; he should act, and does not act. Not being able to act, he lacks honor. The sense of failed honor is a symptom of Hamlet's neurosis, which appears in his agonized contemplation of Fortinbras' Polish venture. Hamlet knows that this rash Norwegian, making mouths at the event, is afflicted by a disease of ambition in fighting for an eggshell. But Hamlet knows, too, that Fortinbras has an honor wanting in himself.

The Henry plays are a catharsis for this neurosis attaching to the name of honor. The catharsis is reached in several ways. There is, first of all, the ridicule of the divinity of kings, the frailty of Richard, and the inflated claims of Glendower. Then there is the pitiless inquisition by Falstaff, along with Hal's own scorn for the impulsive Hotspur. Above all there is old Henry's confession, baring his royal masquerade. Finally, out of all this mutual reduction emerges the figure of Hal attaining a public honor won through private examination of a cause to which he commits his subjects. It is an honor set upon a choice of policy

which must be realized in historical and public time. Yet,
however Hal redeems the time by finding his identity in
political history, the fact remains that politics may not be
enough, for politics and ethics are still at odds, especially
when seen against the theatricality of the Grand Mechanism—a mechanism that looks like idiocy when projected
against ahistorical time.

III

Lived Time and Thought Time:
The Privileged Moment

TIME AND SPACE IN DRAMA

With his dying words Hotspur lessons Hal that thought's
the slave of life, and life time's fool. Which is to say that life
is lived, not thought; or, as the Player King remarks in
Hamlet, "our devices still are overthrown" because "our
thoughts are ours, their ends none of our own." What we
intend is often frustrated, since

> Purpose is but the slave to memory,
> Of violent birth but poor validity.

Indeed, the whole speech of the Player King is filled with
this sort of existential, or tragic, wisdom:

> What to ourselves in passion we propose,
> The passion ending, doth the purpose lose.

Passion gives life its velocity, purpose being an index of
that velocity. Animals do not have purpose in this fully
human sense of the term, for human purpose is a desire to
escape the present; it arises from vision of a future and our
awareness of some possibility of realizing that future.[1]
With conscious purpose the human being enters human
time, a by-product of desire or will. Schopenhauer made
the point that the world in which we exist is a creation of

our will or idea. And Camus reaffirmed, in perhaps another
sense, that man is a creature who refuses to be what he is.
The gap between the present moment and the envisioned
future provokes a consciousness of time, the private direction that is our way of internalizing our world. So each
man has his own temporal horizon, and there is no objective measure of this lived time, scaled by our own values of
urgency or boredom.

The classic discussion of human time is the eleventh
chapter of Augustine's *Confessions,* which asks what measure we can use to reckon the intervals of time. None, he
decides, for "time is nothing else than protraction; but of
what, I know not; and I marvel, if it be not of the mind
itself." We can measure the motion of a body in space but
not the passage of time in the mind. Writing in his *Journal*
on November 16, 1864, Amiel rephrases the Augustinian
problem in modern terms: "Time is the supreme illusion.
It is nothing but the inner prism through which we diffract
being and life." About a year later (August 8, 1865) he adds,
"Time is thus the successive dispersion of being." This
dispersal takes the form that we call experience, in a
rhythm that Francis Fergusson calls tragic "purpose, passion, perception."

In his discussion of the child's mentality, Jean Piaget
notes that "psychologically time depends on velocity," and
therefore cannot be given abstract geometric form, as is the
case with spatial perception. That is, space can be concep-
tualized in absolute form as time cannot. In contrast to the
pure geometry of spatial form, there is no pure or abstract
chronometry, for when time is abstracted, "it becomes a
simple order of succession": "space can be completely abstracted from its content in the measure of pure form," but
"time cannot be abstracted from its content as space can."[2]
The only measure of psychological time is duration, and
duration is not "a simple order of succession."

Upon this distinction Henri Bergson based his treatment

of time: when we try to think time, we must spatialize it into a sequence of hours, days, years; but when we live time (i.e., experience time) it cannot be measured into a schematic succession of past, present, future. Relationships in space are, therefore, more capable of being rationalized than relations in time. The only time that can be rationalized is chronometric time; but the time which is ours in lived experience (which Bergson calls duration) has a rhythm of intensities and measures that evade chronological sequence.

Significantly, the father of modern rationalism, Descartes, resorted to a geometric method which was hardly successful in coping with time. Descartes was forced to deal with time as only a mode of our thinking, whereas space has objective existence:

> Some of the attributes are in things themselves and others are only in our thought. Thus time, for example, . . . is only a mode of thinking . . . ; in order to comprehend the duration of all things under the same measure, we usually compare their duration with the duration of the greatest and most regular motions, which are those that create years and days and these we term time. (*Principles of Philosophy*, Principle LVII)

But durative time, lived time, is obviously not represented by the external coding of days and years, and Descartes cannot measure psychic time by this serial absolute.

In treating absolute time as a steady flow, as if in the mind of God, Newton rationalized time in much the same way. Through Newton's influence the so-called age of reason, the 18th century, was spatially-minded in its vision of the firmament on high. Since space can be thought as time cannot be thought, the enlightenment could conceive of a vast chain of being, originating in God and descending through ethereal and human beings to what no eye can see. Even the political theory of the period, depending upon the concept of a natural order, was based upon a spatial equation, a contractual relationship modelled on a state of nature. This state, as Locke remarked, never existed in history (in time) but in the mind of man. The politics of the enlightenment were essentially spatial. It was left for the 19th century, with its sense of *Zeitgeist*, to bring in the historical method. One of the persistent dilemmas of 19th-century thought was the conflict, especially in liberalism, between the abstract, essentially spatial, premises of its political theory and the growing historical and temporal sense of social evolution, which involved the time dimension.

Georges Poulet's *Studies in Human Time* traces the development of the modern time sense in literature. The Middle Ages set the temporal against the eternal, for all was seen *sub specie aeternitatis*. The world, so far as it was a real world, "was a world of abiding things." This atemporal essence of Being was symbolized in medieval art by the gold background of the triptych, locking the figures of deity, saint, and donor in a changeless light without cast shadow, and these figures existed only insofar as they were embraced by this eternal illumination.

By contrast, the Renaissance began to exist in a world of momentary vicissitude, where light in painting was no longer a constant illumination of Being but a local and secular effect, changing with the hours and cast from a given source inside or outside the scene, the candlelight, for example, that plays over the figures in Georges LaTour's episodes, modifying all features by its flicker. Leonardo wanted to catch the look of things in the ambiguous chiaroscuro of twilight. This sensitivity to the passing appearance, to the fugitive and personal impression of existence, qualified all spatial relationships, subordinating form and matter to atmospheric tone, as in Leonardo's silent vistas against which his figures appear. Space seems a contingency or reflex of a transient subjective vision. Then, finally, in Impressionism space dissolves in the dispersal of form in a tremolo of color and a certain quality of light.

The art of time, with its nongeometry, culminated in the music of the Proustian novel (l'édifice immense du souvenir). As Poulet says, Proustian time is a texture of "fragments and spaces between fragments, of eclipses and anachronisms" structured only by psychic rhythms, counterpointing themes into a symphonic mode where time is felt, not thought, where the cadence is not of events in the external world but immersed in the fluctuation of desire, disillusion, and the slowed velocity of revery, or of disease.

Thus in our modern world time is a fourth dimension in which one cannot order experience spatially. Proustian time is a study in interpenetrations of feelings and perceptions that Descartes could not deal with by his geometric thought. The Proustian novel is not a geometry of experience but a topology having only the rotational symmetry of psychic arcs, of private relationships, of privileged moments. The modern novel, with its associations, dislocations, interruptions, and imprecisions, gives fiction the velocity of the dream as in Robbe-Grillet's fictions where temporal relations are lived confusedly and have little to do with serial chronology or the spatial logic of now, then, next, before, after. Amid the suspensions of a Robbe-Grillet novel the phrase *peut-être* is of importance: "But she is then (immediately afterward or a little later?) facing him, both of them standing in a dark corner of the room, motionless and mute. . . ."[3] The precise mechanical sequences of the old novel have gone, and we are left groping in a duration that defies chronometry. This durative time had already appeared in the 18th-century reverie, a mode of experience dissolving the course of linear time.

In all such cases tempo is more significant than chronology. The Shakespearean play is often an arena where the theatrical time of plot is at discord with the psychic time

we have called duration. Plot is essentially a spatial construct, a design of events, with a causal scheme of beginning, middle, and end (initial situation, complicating incident, rising action, climax, and dénouement). This plot
design does not really trace back to Aristotle, whose *mythos*
is not exactly like our "plot." In Greek drama the velocities
of passion, especially in Euripides, often give rise to the
same kind of intense moments that we so often find in
Shakespearian plays, for both the Greeks and Shakespeare
were willing to sacrifice the logic of plot to the exploitation
of psychic crises which the plot structure hardly justifies.
Then too, as Jacqueline de Romilly says, the anxious memory of the past brings into Euripides a psychic time that
qualifies the mechanics of events.

Thus the chronometric succession of events is a theatrical vehicle often at odds with the psychic or durative tempo
which is the truly dramatic measure of a Shakespearian
play. This conflict between theatrical and dramatic time
has caused irrelevant questions about "double" or
"stretched" time: how long did it take Othello to sail from
Venice to Cyprus; how long did it take Macbeth to go from
Forres to Dunsinane; how old was Hamlet when Yorick
fondled him? Dramatic time, in contrast to theatrical time,
is the changing velocity of endured experience, making
thought the slave of life. Dramatic time is the shift in pace
when Hamlet, having worked himself into a towering rage
to fat kites with his uncle's offal, then cools to the consider-
ation that he should not kill Claudius now, while he prays.
These discontinuities or reversals cannot be accommodated to the logic of plot, which is sequential.

We may need to rephrase G. Wilson Knight's proposal
that a Shakespearian play should be seen "spatially" as an
expansion of certain images. Knight suggests that we experience a Shakespearian drama in space as well as in time,
for by attending to the temporal sequence alone, we lose
the correspondences that create a design extraneous to the

time sequence of the story. It is true that the drama is a form of expanded metaphor—to that extent the plays are spatial. Yet a further distinction is advisable, for if there is a spatial pattern of metaphor, giving the play its "atmosphere," there is also a spatial pattern of plot, since plot is a way of geometrizing time, organizing it into a temporal sequence, as Bergson noted. And lived time cannot be spatialized into a consecutive progression—and then, and then, and then. The psychic drama is lived in discontinuous crises; in contrast to the theatrical sequence of plot, the times are always out of joint, and tempo instead of time becomes an index of experience. The plot is merely the exoskeleton of dramatic intensities.

Thus there are two sorts of spatial design in Shakespeare: the spatializing pattern of recurring metaphors, giving the play its "atmosphere," and the more mechanical spatializing design of plot. The former conveys the texture of lived experience, the "poetry"; the latter is a coordination of events into a chronological succession. The first represents the incoherence or discontinuity or fusions of lived time, or duration; the latter is narration—and for Aristotle, plot or *mythos* is not the same as narrative.

We no longer need to stress the deficiencies of the well-made play, for we accept what Shaw said about plot—that it is a mere executive feat. The fallacies of plot were detected by E. M. Forster in speaking of fiction generally: "The plot, then, is the novel in its logical intellectual aspect." The plot, he says, "is a narrative of events, the emphasis falling on causality."[4] Cause and effect is a kind of rational closure, resulting in the artifice of an "ending." Why, Forster asks, cannot the novel open out instead of going off at the end? Forster charges that the novel borrowed plot from the drama and "the spatial limitations of the stage." One must add not from Shakespeare's stage, for Shakespeare handled plot cavalierly, and was seldom limited by what Forster calls prearrangements: "All that is prearranged is false." (This could have been written by Bergson.) Shakespeare was willing at any moment to sacrifice the logic of plot for psychic crisis.

A great deal of misbegotten effort goes into studying the mechanism of events in Shakespeare's plays. The evil consequences of this inquiry become apparent when questions arise about the "motives" of characters, who are then used as instruments for sustaining the logic of plot. One must not mock Andrew Bradley, who realized that the substance of Shakespearian drama is not plot, but "character." Yet Bradley raised embarrassing questions when he became involved in the chronology of plot: "Where was Hamlet at the time of his father's death?," "When was the murder of Duncan first plotted?," "Did Emilia suspect Iago?" Bradley tried to deal with Shakespeare's characters as if they resembled those we meet daily; thus he did not allow for the illogicalities and discontinuities in the most intense Shakespearean experience.[5] The expected contours of Shakespeare's characters often disintegrate under the pressure of "privileged moments" (the phrase is Bergson's).[6]

Some of the most intense human responses in the plays occur without there being any consistent, or even logical, motive behind them, and instants of great psychic power are expressed in characters who are not entitled to such moments. The most appalling speech that may ever have been written upon death is suddenly unaccountably put in the mouth of Claudio, that mediocre and unrealized personage in *Measure for Measure*, who without any foregoing indication that he has the capacity for such response exclaims:

> Ay, but to die, and go we know not where,
> To lie in cold obstruction and to rot,
> This sensible warm motion to become
> A kneaded clod . . .
>   . . . 'tis too horrible (III, 1)

Such quaking, vulnerable terror we expect of Hamlet, perhaps, but not of Claudio; yet as Muriel Bradbrook says, Shakespeare is always ready to seize a chance for maximum emotional display apart from the "logical framework of events." Again, that negligible, even sordid Prince Clarence, who is about to be butchered in the Tower, bursts, without antecedent indication, into a poetry that belongs in *The Tempest*, not *Richard III*. There is nothing in Clarence's nature to warrant his lyrical sea vision—the fearful wrecks, the thousand men that fishes gnaw upon:

> Wedges of gold, great anchors, heaps of pearl,
> Inestimable stones, unvalued jewels,
> All scattered in the bottom of the sea:
> Some lay in dead men's skulls, and in the holes
> Where eyes did once inhabit, there were crept,
> As 'twere in scorn of eyes, reflecting gems,
> That wooed the slimy bottom of the deep
> And mocked the dead bones that lay scatter'd by. (I, 4)

Some of the most penetrating incursions into human experience are in the mouths of persons ineligible to exhibit these experiences. The asinine trapped Malvolio cries pathetically, "I am not mad, Sir Topas. I say to you this house is dark." Every play has such privileged moments, rebellions against the consistency of character and logic of plot. With his appetite for unwonted response Shakespeare affirms the illuminations rather than the logic of life. If his plots represent a kind of necessity, the privileged moments represent a kind of freedom pressing against the mechanism of event. So the plot or scaffolding of episodes demonstrates a logic of thought time, whereas the privileged moments are a breakthrough into the quality of lived time, a transformation of character inaccessible to logic or expectation.

However firmly they may be plotted, the plays usually treat plot as an accessory to the freedom of human consciousness. Especially in later plays like *Cymbeline* the drama is increasingly open to mutations of character that cannot be explained by foregoing events or any pattern of cause and effect. *Cymbeline* depends upon the indeterminations of the moral life. There are many reversals in the course of events in this play, but these reversals are of secondary importance to the privileged moments, as when Posthumus, for no accountable reason, makes his wager with the yellow Iachimo that Imogen can be seduced. Conversely, there is no reason why forgiveness should be so freely bestowed by Antony on Cleopatra, or by Prospero on those who have injured him. No clinical psychology can adequately explain the unmotivated jealousy of Leontes in *The Winter's Tale;* his hatred and suspicion are offered entirely out of context.

There are few privileged moments in a play like *Comedy of Errors,* dominated as it is by a scheme of episodes organized as if in spatial design, into a rectangle of accidents that pass for fate. This neat design of events prearranged in linear time sequence requires Shakespeare to impose on human experience a highly rationalized grid of coincidence, itself a paradox, since coincidence ceases to be coincidence when such mischances are cast into this prearrangement. The essential inhumanity of the play is immediately implied in the speech of Solinus, Duke of Ephesus, who tells the unfortunate Egeon that he cannot infringe laws sealed to exclude pity:

> Therefore by law thou art condemned to die . . .
> For we may pity, though not pardon thee. (I, 1)

The very imagery of the play is dominated by equations, as when Egeon recounts the shipwreck in which his family were divided:

> Our helpful ship was splitted in the midst,
> So that, in this unjust divorce of us,

> Fortune hath left to both of us alike,
> What to delight in, what to sorrow for. (I, 1)

So far as time operates in this play, it must be synchronized. Antipholus of Syracuse must at a given instant meet Dromio of Ephesus, or vice versa. But these are only the superficial manifestations of time in life. The more significant infiltration of time into human experience is not in a diagram of events but, instead, in what Bergson calls the gnawing of time, the interpenetrations of past and present with future, the disturbed moments when Hamlet sees what he has been, and is, and should be. Hamlet's experience in time is asynchronic.

The artificiality of a synchronic view of time is suggested in *As You Like It*, not only in Rosalind's exchange with Orlando (III, 2) on "who Time ambles withal, who Time trots withal, who Time gallops withal, and who he stands still withal," but, more specifically, in the scheme of life phrased in Jaques's discourse on the seven ages of man (II, 7), translating experience into a sequence of roles we each play in turn, a mere succession of entrances and exits from infancy to age—a preposterous falsification in light of Hamlet's concurrent roles, enacted in a durative experience that is existential anguish.[7] Hamlet does not know who he is; his roles are multiple, usually contradictory. So are Macbeth's, for Macbeth is torn between his moral and criminal roles, which he plays simultaneously and idiotically, much like Othello. Claudius does not have the human privilege or anguish of undergoing this stress of conflicting roles, which make Macbeth live in tension between evil and good.

The dramatic or privileged moment involves anachronism. Othello, for example, reveals this anachronism ironically when he addresses Desdemona just before Iago causes him to believe she is a whore:

> Excellent wretch! Perdition catch my soul
> But I do love thee! and when I love thee not,
> Chaos is come *again*. (III, 3)

Surely there is no more tragic use of the adverb *again* in all
literature for the chaos is already there, as the Moor seems
unconsciously to know. This anachronism in the human
condition is waived in the serial time of plot if by plot we
mean a sequence of narrative episodes arranged to focus at
a climax. Dramatic psychology requires an illogical montage of the phases of time we separate factitiously into past,
present, and future.

In his mature dramas Shakespeare does not schematize
time by typecasting his characters into the successive roles
reviewed in Jaques's speech on the ages of man. Cleopatra,
that serpent of old Nile who is wrinkled deep in time, is a
creature that age cannot wither; her most mature role is a
return to the youthful innocence of a maid doing meanest
chores. Her infinite variety which stimulates while it cloys
indicates how specious is Jaques's classification of the
course of age—or at least how it belies Shakespeare's dramatic and discontinuous uses of time. Young as he is, Hamlet with his prophetic soul is prematurely sage.

This asynchronic or asequential time is the vehicle of
endured experience. In his most penetrating drama Shakespeare is aware of the mysterious, illogical discontinuities
and reversals of time, for durative time cannot be plotted.
Continuity belongs to plot, discontinuity to character. Everyone speaks of the parallels between the major and the
sustaining plots in *Lear*; but the substance of *Lear* is not in
these homologous plots. It is, instead, in the imbecility of
age, the wearing out of life, the perverted capitulation of
parent to child, or the abnormality inhering in an act of
generation that should secure the future. The full triumph
of asynchronic over synchronic time comes when Antony
and Cleopatra are projected by their lust from the domain

of history into an envisioned Elysium, and when Prospero refuses to exact penalty for the wrongs of the past by an act of pardon that cancels the demands of time through a gesture of virtue, not vengeance.

We know from the sonnets how Shakespeare felt the burden of lived time, which seemed to him almost like fate itself. The sonnets suggest that Shakespeare, like any Renaissance man, had a time perspective that the middle ages would not have understood. He sees how Time's hand defaces brass and the rich monuments of the past. He knows how the hungry ocean inevitably gains on the shore, and that time will take his love away. The modern scientist speaks of the unidirectional flow of time, which is irreversible, obeying a law of entropy; and Shakespeare laments that gates of steel are not impregnable against the siege of days. The closing couplets of these mighty sonnets on time are strangely ineffectual, almost a triviality or witticism— the protest that his love will still shine bright in ink, and that beauty will endure in his praise of it. All such claims are a pretense that would encounter the ravage of time by a feat of art. But Shakespeare knew as well as Milton that fame is an infirmity of the noble mind.

THE PRIVILEGED MOMENT

The futility of the mind as an instrument to govern human experience is the theme of that early but mature play, *Love's Labour's Lost*, which begins and ends with a testing of life by time.[8] The King of Navarre, establishing his little Academe still and contemplative in the art of living, proclaims with Renaissance vanity that the mind can master the affections and huge desires of the world—the fame that lives registered on brazen tombs can bate the edge of devouring Time. Those in the Academe have attempted to arrest the course of time by isolating themselves from passion, which Berowne says is mutable. Berowne knows from the first how foolish it is to suppose that the mind can banquet though the body pine, and he predicts that fleshly necessity will make these dandies forsworn long before the three-year term of their oath to fast, to study, not to sleep, or to see women:

> For every man with his affects is born,
> Not by might mast'red, but by special grace. (I, 1)

(Berowne is making Bergson's point that "all morality is in essence biological.") An oddity in this foppish play is the constant appearance of the term *grace*, indicating that we do not of ourselves have full control of our fate.

Though presumably written for a sophisticated audience, perhaps for one of Southampton's fetes at Titchfield, the play astonishingly moves "beyond culture." It is a severe examination of the ambitions of official humanism—"learning," says Berowne, "is but an adjunct to ourself." (IV,3) Even more notable, the play, presumably written about 1593–1594, anticipates what Francis Bacon some decade later wrote about the need to destroy the idols of the mind by appealing to the true induction from experience. Bacon set about demolishing fantastical, delicate, and contentious learning, rejecting the vanities of cloistered study and the victories of wit. The mind, said Bacon, is a magnificent structure without foundation except in experience, and the world is not to be narrowed to fit the reason, which should be expanded until it can accept the world as it is in fact. "So it is in contemplation; if a man will begin with certainties, he shall end in doubts, but if he will begin with doubts, he shall end in certainties." The insanity of the academic program leads Berowne to protest, "As true we are as flesh and blood can be," thus endorsing John Keats's pragmatic belief that "axioms in philosophy are not axioms until they are proved upon our pulses."

The folly of attempting to master life by the mind is revealed at each social level of the play, for like the nobles, Don Armado the autodidact, falls in love with Jacquenetta while Costard, the hind, having also been enchanted by this lowly damsel, exclaims in nearly Biblical language, "Such is the simplicity of man to hearken after the flesh." It takes a little longer for Berowne to be seduced by Rosaline, the dark lady, and to decide that he must lose his oath to find himself. For while Berowne had earlier seen that men are victims of change and time, he has had the overweening confidence that he is exempt from the casualties of love. When he does fall in love with Rosaline, he is betrayed into a profession of constancy that is a denial of time: "to thee I'll faithful prove." Rosaline cures him of this self-assurance, and the play closes with a jarring submission to the uncertainties of lived time, the testing of his wit for a year amid the dying.

In short, the little Academe was originally an attempt to deny time and to make its members "heirs of all eternity" by a cultural puritanism warring against affections and "the huge army of the world's desires," especially love. But when the four do fall in love, they still deny time by striking the pose of constancy. Then comes the news of the King of France's death, a grim evidence of the extremity of time's rage, and Berowne is the first to recognize that the scene begins to cloud. The clouds will linger as Rosaline sends Berowne to jest with the mortally ill—"to move wild laughter in the throat of death." We do not know how successful Berowne will be, and the play ends with a contingent future. Jack hath not Jill, and may never have Jill if the testing fails. The deeply lived experience is all ahead. The little Academe was a closure; the prospects at the end are all open, or provisional.

In *Two Sources of Morality and Religion* Bergson contrasts the closed society with the open. The closed society is essentially inhuman, its members bound in an order protecting it against change, against the uncertainties of social mobility and unwonted responses. The open society embraces men and their possibilities more widely, able as it is to accommodate changes that defy expectation; it is like "a dream dreamt," receptive to the "unceasing transformation" that accedes to the verifications of expanding experience, to the mutations of time.

In *Love's Labour's Lost* there is a native antagonism between Berowne, whose future is open, and Boyet, "the ape of form, monsieur the nice," whose future can be no different from his present. Boyet the courtier lives by his code of manners which is his only resource, making him ineligible for the expanding experiences of Berowne, who is chastened and instructed by Rosaline. Boyet is exempt from any changes time might work on him. His role has been cast once and for all, and he cannot be touched by the larger grace bestowed on Berowne when he is humbled.

Boyet lives by an orthodoxy that seems to have been increasingly abhorrent to Shakespeare. For orthodoxy is an arrest of time, or, to use Bergson's phrase, a codification of life prohibiting the mutations requisite in an open society, the sensitivity to time that allows creative exfoliations of experience. With his easy compliance Boyet has his own kind of malleability, for he is at everybody's service and is concessive to every occasion, a master of apt phrase and gesture, without, however, being touched by any failures. Berowne is sadly disconcerted by his reverses; but though he loses his poise, he learns a great deal from his chagrin. Berowne belongs with Benedick, who, being caught in a trap of his own making in *Much Ado*, responds with a similar adaptability by confessing, "Happy are they that hear their detractions and can put them to mending." Berowne and Benedick can profit by the overturns in experience and can transcend the shock of the unexpected by a new, if painful, recoil. The "honey-tongued" Boyet is not capable of such moral or psychological renovation.

Shakespeare was much concerned with the adaptability making such renovation possible, and his dislike of orthodoxy, codes, and mechanical responses resembles Bergson's kindred distaste. Like Bergson, Shakespeare appreciated the distinctively human faculty to accommodate changing occasions. Indeed, one may take Hamlet to be among the most unorthodox figures in drama, living as he does in the fluctuation of moments, sensitively and even incoherently meeting the changing demands of the instant until his character disintegrates into a discontinuous succession of reactions. More readily than anyone Hamlet accedes to the stimulus of the immediate and lacks any code to deal with it, so he is forever open to the unexpected or unorthodox recoil. He is a creature who mutates with the passing moment, who plunges more deeply than any Shakespearean character into what Carlyle called the time element, or what Heidegger calls *Dasein*.

In contrast to Hamlet's mutations, Shylock is a figure who refuses the meaning of time, which Amiel called a dispersal of being. If Hamlet's being is dispersed into incoherent available responses, Shylock's contour is fixed as a Puritan living by the letter of the law. As an image of orthodoxy Shylock is inflexible, pitiless, and inhuman. He craves the penalties of the bond; there is no power of appeal to alter him. Yet because Shakespeare was always ready to exploit a rhetorical opportunity, there is at moments another Shylock than this Shylock of the arrested image— Shylock the injured one. For Shylock is Janus-faced and has two unrelated contours coexisting. But we never see much of this other injured Shylock since the plot hinges upon the inhuman Puritan Shylock of unyielding and rigid contour.

The pertinence of all this to Bergson's theory of comedy is apparent, for Bergson held that we are human only through our faculty to adapt to the occasion, as if biologically.[9] If our responses are automatic or mechanized, there comes a moment when we are inadequate to meet the unexpected, and we accordingly alienate sympathy by isolating ourselves from the human condition, bringing upon us the penalty of mocking laughter. Bergson treats comedy as a repetition of behavior that is suddenly interrupted. Implicit in this theory is a contrast between space and time: the repeated response is a mechanized pattern of conduct; then comes the instant when this pattern breaks down.

Shylock cannot meet this test, nor can any Puritan, since Puritanism is a stereotyped response, a grid imposed upon our humanity. One reason why we pour contempt upon poor Malvolio is his automatism that is suddenly and disastrously interrupted. But Beatrice and Benedick are able to revise their automatism when they are faced with the critical instant, thus redeeming themselves. Shylock is not eligible for such redemption. His automatism excludes him from his latent humanity, which appears *outside* the logic of the plot when he asks, "If you prick us, do we not bleed?" Shylock as a grotesque and Shylock as a person: Shakespeare is sacrificing Shylock the person to Shylock the grotesque. Secondarily he is a person, not only because of the inviolable integrity of his selfhood, which appears in his query why he should lend Antonio money in the face of insults, but also in his grief at Jessica's exchanging Leah's ring for a monkey. Yet this human Shylock is veiled by Shylock the grotesque—the Shylock who whets his knife and, more unfairly still, the Shylock who is said to wander through the streets crying outrageously:

> My daughter! O my ducats! O my daughter!
> Fled with a Christian! O my Christian ducats!

The contour is there without the person.

Shylock is also the business man, thriving by interest, which is the price of time. In commercial transactions human time—the duration that is qualitative or lived time—is translated into calendar time, which is quantitative. The three thousand ducats loaned for three months schematizes time as Puritanism schematizes response. If the orthodox believer denies the quality of lived time by mechanizing his responses, economic man denies the quality of lived time (which allows mercy) by schematizing it into a chronometric scale of indebtedness. Orthodoxy and interest are instruments for protecting us against the casualties of human time, which is permeated with illogicalities, uncertainties, surprises, discontinuities. In the orthodox and commercial regulation of life there are no privileged moments.

Considering the frivolities of the gentiles in *The Merchant of Venice,* one hesitates to argue that they are more acceptable than Shylock, for Shylock has an integrity that is the more valid aspect of the Puritan. Yet if one disregards the fraudulence of the gentiles, the play exhibits a contrast between Shylock's bondage to orthodox or economic time and the gentile freedom in time. The casket scene in which Bassanio wins Portia is based not upon economic time but upon the fortunate chance, the privileged moment that brings happiness. The return of Antonio's ships is likewise a liberation from economic time, the happy chance that makes insurance irrelevant and secures the future. Then there is the mercy that should be given at a blessed instant demanding the abrogation of law, a privileged moment like grace bestowed. Doubtless Shakespeare did not consider all this; but the play can be read as dealing with two orders of time, an opposition of justice with mercy, orthodoxy with humanity, necessity with freedom. Justice is an equation; mercy is an incommensurate act.

The same contrasts recur in *Measure for Measure,* where there is another way of controlling time—by authority. The Duke stands in the background manipulating by his hidden will the destiny of others. The play is Calvinist insofar as it demonstrates the operation of inscrutable power; and it is Puritan insofar as it studies orthodox mentality and conduct. Both questions bear upon freedom and necessity. So far as the fates of the characters are subject to the will of invisible authority, there is only necessity, or rather, there is freedom for the hidden agent and necessity for those he manipulates. In this sense only the Duke is free. But there is another meaning of freedom—the freedom that comes when at a privileged moment Angelo and Isabella release themselves from the bondage of orthodoxy and begin to live authentically as human beings who have seen their inadequacies and have undertaken to mend them. In their orthodoxy they are shackled in time; in their self-examination they are free in time, for at the critical instant they unshackle themselves from their mechanical codes and change their lives.

Like *The Merchant of Venice* this play is about the law, the biting statutes by which Isabella and Angelo at first live, and about the arbitrary will of the Duke. Angelo and Isabella are Puritan in the most severe sense of the term; their existence is regulated by a rigidity of behavior and thought that guards them against the perils of lived time. Abiding by the letter, they abdicate their freedom to respond. "It is the law, not I, condemn your brother," says Angelo (II, 2) to Isabella, who herself has lived by the law, as she remarks to Lucio:

> . . . I speak not as desiring more,
> But rather wishing a more strict restraint
> Upon the sisterhood. (I, 4)

This reliance upon extreme orthodoxy causes Isabella to say, "More than our brother is our chastity." (II, 4) Both she and Angelo exhibit a frigidity lacking in Shylock, who always has the capacity for passionate response. Isabella and Angelo are more completely automated. It is curious too that Isabella should be the first to encourage Angelo to play with the law. In this she is at one with the Duke, who has evasively waived the laws against lechery.

Angelo is the first to break out of the orthodox mechanization of life, entering into the perplexity of lived time when he suddenly realizes, by an earthquake in his consciousness, that he is going the way to temptation where prayers cross, where one sins in loving virtue. Distracted as he is by the onset of lust, he finds himself, as Isabella later does, at war between will and will-not. Or, as Bergson has it, when we begin to think about our acts, the meaning of our action reaches our consciousness "only confusedly." This confusion in consciousness never appeared in that other play about orthodoxy, *The Merchant of Venice*. But in one of the great speeches in *Measure for Measure*, Angelo, a far inferior character to Shylock morally, examines the fallacy of orthodoxy and finds that he is lost:

> When I would pray and think, I think and pray
> To several subjects: heaven hath my empty words,
> Whilst my invention, hearing not my tongue,
> Anchors on Isabel: heaven in my mouth,
> As if I did but only chew his name,
> And in my heart the strong and swelling evil
> Of my conception. (II, 4)

It should be noted that although a clinical interpretation is here available, Angelo's experience at this privileged moment transcends the clinical and becomes an ethical crisis with profoundly human meaning.

Isabella does not have her privileged moment until the last scene when she realizes that she is the one who, by her very purity, tempted Angelo: "I partly think," she says,

> A due sincerity governed his deeds
> Till he did look on me.

At this moment she abandons her orthodoxy to accept an ethic of shared guilt, for she sees that the tempter is bracketed in guilt with the tempted. According to the old law of retribution there was a polarity of guilt and innocence, but Isabella perceives that this binary puritan ethic is fallacious since it does not establish a human relation between offender and offended—it is a mere abstraction.

In pleading for Angelo, Isabella intuits a new relation of shared guilt; it is a relation described by Albert Camus in judging that individually we may be innocent but communally we are guilty. According to this humanistic ethic, your guilt is but the reflex of my innocence, and thus I am to a degree responsible for your shortcomings. Angelo is Isabella's hell—a very modern relativism. Isabella's response is as unexpected as it is concessive; she has successfully met the crisis of the instant and entered into a new freedom which is an intimation of the necessity binding me and thee.

By the letter of the law there is an equation: measure for measure. In Isabella's sense of shared guilt this equation breaks down, and she accepts the irrationality of a justice that cannot mete out retribution in any direct proportion to offence. At her privileged moment she invokes the theological value of grace bestowed—the grace which is the recurring theme of the play, touching the question of time as well as freedom from the letter of the law. Calvinists believed that by an arbitrary extension of unearned mercy God can exempt from damnation those upon whom penalty should fall. This release from the law by grace is, so to speak, an *ad hoc* decision on God's part.

The corresponding *ad hoc* exemption in Counter Reformation Romanism was casuistry, that is, manipulating the law in special cases on the basis of foregoing precedents to make penance lighter than it should logically be. Casuistry is the use of an exceptional dispensation. As John Henry Newman explains, an ethical system can supply laws, but "who is to apply them to a particular case?" Newman terms this faculty for applying the inflexible law to the individual case the illative sense, a sense that "determines what science cannot determine," i.e., what suffices in the present instance, at a given moment. Casuistry is the qualification of the law in behalf of the situation at hand. It is an adjustment required by human time. Like the incidence of grace, casuistic exemption is an advantage granted in privileged moments, a suspension of the abiding precept *hic et nunc*, here and now.

In *Measure for Measure* there are two sorts of privileged moments, those that are bestowed and those that are earned, though both give freedom from the law. The manipulations by the Duke represent a freedom that is given, not chosen or earned. The Duke's pardoning of Angelo is an act quite as arbitrary as his original delegation of power or his arranging the bed trick for Mariana. Throughout the action the Duke stands in the wings regulating the course of everyone's fortunes, so that what looks like freedom is actually necessity—in Calvinist phrase, only God is free, whereas man is necessitated. The Duke redeems the time at will. Such autocratic control of fate is a specious conquest of time. According to the Duke's will there is, or there is not (as with Lucio), measure for measure, leading to an evasion of lived time, which should be something more than foreordained.

This sort of irrational fate—the privileged moment in which one is saved or damned by authority—is different from the discontinuity and illogicality of lived human time in which reversals occur without being imposed. As Bergson would say, there is no creative evolution in Calvinist fatality, which depends upon God's will. But there is a profoundly creative evolution in the disturbing experiences of Angelo and Isabella while they are at war "twixt will and will not." The indetermination in their evolution is apparent in their heightening perplexity as they learn about themselves. Their very perplexity is witness of their earned authenticity, their discovery of their selfhood. (Karl Jaspers has said that "selfhood begins with perplexity in face of the real and the possible."[10]) The absurdity of their self-identification is the more striking in that neither character, bound as it was to orthodoxy and to ignorance of the possible, was really eligible for self-redemption. Shylock, with his inherent integrity, was eligible for self-redemption, yet never had the privilege of freeing himself from his orthodoxy so he must simply be expelled. His privileged moments, as when he is most conscious of his exclusion from the gentile society closing in upon him, are never fulfilled in the self-examination that exempts Isabella and Angelo from the mechanism of their orthodoxy, and also from the fatality of the Duke's jurisdiction.

Romeo and Juliet is the play in which there is an imposed fatality. The star-crossed lovers, suffering their "misadventured piteous overthrows," are caught in a design that is diligently spatial in its contrasts: Montagu vs. Capulet, age vs. youth, Rosaline vs. Juliet, Juliet vs. the Nurse, Romeo vs. Paris, Friar Laurence vs. the feuding families, Mercutio, vs. Tybalt and Romeo, episode vs. episode, and the whole carefully measured within and without Verona's walls. Yet even within this mechanism of plot and character there are certain privileged moments that redeem the play as human experience, not Romeo's rhetoric and gesture, but Mercutio's bawdy and, above all, Juliet's anti-puritan love, which accepts the flesh:

> Come, gentle night; come, loving black-browed night;
> Give me my Romeo. . . . (III, 2)

Juliet in her surrender to passion represents all that is anti-Platonic, all that is at odds with the highfalutin ascetic and academic in *Love's Labour's Lost* or even Shakespeare's own high-flown sonnet on the marriage of true minds. Juliet at this moment embodies a lived experience in human time. She lives by intensities, not continuities; by instants, not by endurance; by reversals, not by security.

These intensities reappear in *Midsummer Night's Dream* when Lysander exclaims that the course of love never runs smoothly:

> War, death, or sickness did lay seige to it,
> Making it momentany as a sound,
> Swift as a shadow, short as any dream,
> Brief as the lightning in the collied night. (I, 1)

This play brings its own strange redemption from chronometric time and geometric plot design. The mechanism of action is as carefully spatialized as it was in *Comedy of Errors:* the two sets of lovers, their changing juxtapositions, and the parallels between different worlds with their answerable confusions. Even the play within the play, the ridiculous Pyramus and Thisby interlude, structurally duplicates the insanity and mischances of the four lovers. Here too is the pressure of law, for Theseus has condemned Hermia either to wed Demetrius or

> to die the death, or to abjure
> For ever the society of men.

Theseus is as autocratic as the Duke Vincentio in *Measure for Measure.*

But there is also a release from this mechanization by the wonder of the dream, a recognition of the incoherence and reversals when life is lived by intensities. The madness of the night is momentary, but its consequences are abiding and curative. In the clear light of the Athenian dawn Demetrius asks whether they wake or sleep, for the events of the night, seeming far off and undistinguishable, nevertheless endow the lovers with a double vision, a sense of redemption from confusion. Hippolyta remarks,

> But all the story of the night told over,
> And all their minds transfigured so together,
> More witnesseth than fancy's images
> And grows to something of great constancy;
> But howsoever strange and admirable. (V,1)

Poor Bottom himself has had his redemptive dream, a most rare vision of being loved by the Fairy Queen, and he affirms that "man is but an ass if he go about to expound this dream." Even the epilogue stresses that the whole action was a vision like slumber, "no more yielding but a dream."

The command of time by this midsummer vision, which is radically unlike the attempt to command life by learning, by asceticism, by law, by orthodoxy, is a testimony of human freedom. One thinks again of Bergson's plea for the opening of life, which comes as "a dream dreamt by chosen souls," embodying "something of itself in creations, each of which through a more or less far-reaching transformation of man, conquers difficulties hitherto unconquerable." The prologue to the Pyramus and Thisby playlet voices this transformation, which is apocalyptic:

> Gentles, perchance you wonder at this show;
> But wonder on, till truth make all things plain. (V, 1)

There are few more privileged moments in Shakespeare until we reach the Prospero vision of life.

IV
Punctual Time:
Hamlet

The idea of the privileged moment reappears in another mode in Gaston Roupnel's *Nouvelle Siloë*. In one of his early books, *L'Intuition de l'instant,* Gaston Bachelard contrasts the view of time taken by Henri Bergson with Roupnel's view of time. Both Bergson and Roupnel regard time as the medium in which we create ourselves. For both, life is a perpetual emergence. The difference between Bergson and Roupnel is that Bergson emphasizes the continuity of change persisting like a flow through a zone of episodic moments, whereas Roupnel emphasizes the discontinuous and unique originality of each instant. Bergson (in *Creative Evolution*) writes:

> A thousand incidents arise, which seem to be cut off from those which precede them, and to be disconnected from those which follow. Discontinuous though they appear, however, in point of fact they stand out against the continuity of a background on which they are designed, and to which indeed they owe the intervals that separate them.

So there is no real difference between "passing from one state to another and persisting in the same state." Bergson sees the flow of our experience as horizontal, each original moment, however privileged or unforeseeable, being an aspect of the duration in which our being is realized.

Roupnel, in reaction against Bergson, proposed that our evolution in time is more episodic: "Time has only one reality, the instant. In other words, time is a reality locked in the moment that is suspended between two nothingnesses," the past and the future. For Roupnel, duration is only a construct of imagination or memory; our lived experience is punctiform rather than continuous. Roupnel sees our evolution occurring in the verticality of the present. As Bachelard says, Bergson has a philosophy of action, Roupnel a philosophy of the act, the instant being more expressive and inventive than duration. Thus while Bergson and Roupnel alike accept an organic or genetic view of human experience, Bergson detects the continuity of life and Roupnel its interruptions. Here is a contrast between time in *Macbeth* and time in *Hamlet*.

In his chapter on "Le Problème de l'Habitude et le Temps Discontinu," Bachelard prefers Roupnel to Bergson—if life is the habit of being, expressing itself in a sustained rhythm, yet repetition does not destroy the novelty of the instant. Each instant is, to be sure, a mode of repetition, but it is also a commencement. Bachelard agrees that the uniqueness of every instant is a crisis giving time its vertical quality, standing out against the horizontal coherence of duration. For Bachelard the poem is a crisis of the instant, a monument to a present moment, a symbol of time in its punctiform originality. The poem validates each commencement. And for Bachelard each truly moral act is punctiform: "all morality is instantaneous," emerging vertically in all its own vitality. When we act morally, says Bachelard, we break the bounds of habitude: "Suddenly the horizontal flatness vanishes. Le temps ne coule plus. Il jaillit." Time vibrates.

With his usual ambiguity and detachment Shakespeare may be said to deal in *Hamlet* with the nature of Roupnel's punctiform time, then in *Macbeth* with the nature of Bergsonian durative time.

At the very start of the play Hamlet is faced with the problems of punctual time. Having seen his father's ghost, he is jolted out of the coherence that durative time can give life:

> Yes, from the table of my memory
> I'll wipe away all trivial fond records,
> All saws of books, all forms, all pressures past
> That youth and observation copied there . . . (I, 5)

His life becomes a succession of agonizing instants, each a commencement deprived of the wonted context of the past.

The punctiform time in *Hamlet* is related to "one of the most important turning points in the history of science and technology, indeed of all human art and culture," namely, the invention of the clock, an instrument that brought a new consciousness of discontinuous time into Renaissance experience. Until the Renaissance the usual instrument for measuring time was the water clock or the hourglass, devices that could not divide time into minutes or seconds.[1] Time flowed, but it was not punctiform, could not be parceled into moments. The invention of the escapement made possible the mechanical clock, which broke up the durative flow of time into critical intervals that eventually made inevitable the machinery of the Newtonian physics. As Joseph Needham says of the clock, "The problem was to find a way of slowing down the rotation of a set of wheels (an escapement, in fact) so that it would keep step with the great clock of the skies, that apparent diurnal rotation of the heavens which star-clerks and astronomers had studied since the beginning of civilization."

While indicated by the sun dial and such devices, time flowed "naturally" and continuously, but not in the accurately designated intervals available after the invention of the escapement, which evidently appeared at the end of the 13th century and was perfected in the 17th. By means of the verge escapement or the pallet escapement of the pendulum clock the whole concept of time was affected through the counting of mechanical oscillations, each fractioning time into a new rhythm of "present" instants. The escapement clock "constituted perhaps the greatest tool of the Scientific Revolution of the seventeenth century . . . and it furnished a philosophical model for the world picture which grew up on the basis of the 'analogy of mechanism.' " Newton's idea of the uniform flow of absolute time may, indeed, be a residue of the old continuous time of the hourglass or water clock, whereas his idea of local times may derive from the escapement clock.

Hamlet stands on a boundary between a world where time was a natural and indivisible flow—when the sidereal rhythms of the macrocosm and the civil time of due succession were the usual measures—and the post-Renaissance world with its sense of punctual, mechanical time. For him the time is out of joint in a very deep sense. The mechanics of the cosmos had already appeared in the Copernican vision, and Hamlet's conduct shows some of the behavioristic reactions of a later psychology.

Almost by prescience Hamlet's experiences show the crisis brought into Renaissance culture by the sense of punctiform time, for his life develops discontinuously, deprived of coherence after he returns to Denmark, where he is disturbed by thoughts beyond the reaches of his soul. He cannot reconcile his conflicting instantaneous responses, and the whole play is a study in interrupted or punctiform reactions. Hamlet's psychology is "situational," for he exists, thinks, feels in a succession (not a sequence) of critical moments in which he comes face to face with those persons who elicit, as he faces them, violently contradictory emotions. His "character" is, in fact, a succession of responses to rapidly changing stimuli, a succession of recoils and sympathies *vis à vis* the figures who rotate, scene by scene, about him, each provoking a crisis in consciousness: Ophelia, Gertrude, Claudius, Polonius, Fortinbras, Horatio,

Rosencrantz and Guildenstern, and the pirates and the gravedigger. And these responses do not always seem to be in his control.

One might say that Hamlet as a character has only a negative identity, shifting and even disintegrating into the discontinuities induced by these crises in response. He illustrates what Brecht implied when he stated that the continuity of the ego is a myth. A psychologist would say that Hamlet suffers from personality diffusion. Unpredictable, frequently violent, incoherent, his selfhood is an answer to the demands made upon his acute sensibility instant by instant. Hamlet is everyone—and no one. Potentially he is aesthete, Borgia, scholar, courtier, lover, romantic, cynic, and dandy. Most of the characters about him are his alter egos: Horatio is Hamlet's (inaccessible) honest self; Polonius is his (rejected) respectable self; Claudius is his (rejected) Borgia self; Fortinbras is his (rejected) princely activist self; Osric is his (rejected) foppish self; the players and pirates are his (congenial) bohemian self. Until his last moments Hamlet exists largely by his refusals and negations, and the drama is like a hall of distorting mirrors through which he passes catching momentary reflections of a self that reaches identity only at death. Hamlet's experience is punctiform, episodically distributed through acts that do not, until the end, cohere into action.

Hamlet's difficulty is to give some stability to this discontinuous experience which neither logic nor feeling can unify. The intense meaning of one moment has, he finds, nothing to do with the intense meaning of the preceding or following moment. His paralysis is a symptom of his capacity to over-respond to the occasion. In one way the key to the play is not given by Hamlet but by Polonius, who says that we find our direction only by indirections, by windlasses and assays of bias. Hamlet has an overriding need of direction, of equilibrium and continuity in a life that has collapsed into dissonant crises. Time for Hamlet

lacks horizontality; it vibrates; each instant is a commencement, stimulating him to reactions that are sensitive yet
mechanical. In the whirlwind of his passionate responses
he finds in Horatio and the players what he most seeks,
poise and temperance, which can make time cohere.

The play is an exploration of various ways to bring time
into joint, to impose some continuity and coherence upon
the anachronisms: Claudius popping into the succession,
the law's delay, the premature ageing of Hamlet, the child-
ishness of the adult Polonius, the passions smoldering in
bones of a mature Gertrude, the wearing away of purpose,
the posthaste in a land that makes Sunday like a weekday,
the corruption of the bud before it flowers, the overhasty
marriage of Gertrude, and above all the disrelationship of
Hamlet's successive moments.

The play is, from his point of view, an examination of the
various means of giving coherence to time, chiefly by plotting, by habit or custom, by the ritual of art or role-playing,
and, finally, by improvising or accepting the moment as it
comes, that is, yielding to time instead of trying to command it through the preceding methods.

As has been said of *Hamlet*, everyone plots, and everyone
fails. To plot is to venture to command the course of time
by a logic intended to secure the future. The logic of plot
is nearly syllogistic: if one does this, then certain consequences follow. To plot is to envision foreseen ends, and all
plotting is future-oriented. A successful plot requires a
kind of insensitivity to chance, even though Claudius realizes more vividly than Hamlet or Polonius that there are as
many abatements as there are accidents. The poise of the
accomplished plotter is apparent in Claudius's first speech
from the throne when he shows that his discretion has
fought with nature and mastered it. He can not only think
but even speak openly of his murder with "wisest sorrow,"
with an "auspicious and a dropping eye" enabling him to
weigh precisely delight and dole, holding in judicious bal-

ance his mirth in funeral and dirge in marriage. One of the most appalling implications in *Hamlet*, incidentally, is Claudius's immovable sanity. Though he acknowledges his guilt in the prayer scene, he suffers few of the moral disturbances that afflict Hamlet, who, like Angelo, *feels* his guilt. The contrast between Hamlet's tormented Puritan sense of being sullied and Claudius's invulnerability to his conscience suggests that there is an unbridgeable gap between sanity and moral sensitivity. Claudius is largely immune to the perplexities of the moral life; his mind is not tainted.

Hamlet plots, and in his very plotting has a relish that Claudius does not enjoy. It is sweet to him "When in one line two crafts directly meet," and he has an unholy satisfaction in presenting the Mouse Trap and in the ingenuity of his fabricated letter sending Rosencrantz and Guildenstern to death, for they do not touch his conscience. Then at the last his plots pall. But with his anguished moral imagination he is instinctively repelled by Claudius's coarseness and assurance, the complete efficiency of this Borgia-like politician. Like Iago or Lady Macbeth, Claudius has made life subservient to his will. He would reason his way to the future by his vicious plans. He will provide, he tells Laertes, not one but two devices for liquidating Hamlet, the poisoned foil and the poisoned cup. By criminal foresight he gives time coherence, untroubled by thoughts beyond the reaches of his soul. His purpose has clarified his existence.

Hamlet's sense of the hiatuses in time, with its wicked speed, is in contrast to Claudius's speech on the death of fathers as the common theme in nature:

> But you must know your father lost a father,
> That father lost, lost his. (I, 2)

"This must be so," says Claudius, and grief must have a term lest the mind seem impatient and unschooled.

Claudius is able to make his most impulsive act appear to suit a continuity of events, for when he determines to exile Hamlet, he remarks:

> To bear all smooth and even,
> This sudden sending him away must seem
> Deliberate pause. (IV, 3)

Claudius understands the disjointures of time far better than Hamlet, and is not disconcerted, as Hamlet is, by the falling off of purpose in the erratic course of events. With his consummate sanity Claudius is able to cope with time's reversals, for he advises Laertes:

> . . . I know love is begun by time,
> And that I see, in passages of proof,
> Time qualifies the spark and fire of it.
> There lives within the very flame of love
> A kind of wick or snuff that will abate it,
> And nothing is at a like goodness still . . .
> . . . That we would do
> We should do when we would, for this "would" changes,
> And hath abatements and delays as many
> As there are tongues, are hands, are accidents. (IV, 7)

By this cynical comprehension of time Claudius is able to command the instant as Hamlet is not.

Yet this policy results in a paralysis that is not entirely unrelated to Hamlet's paralysis. Claudius is immobilized in a frigidity that exhibits itself in the chapel scene. He knows that his offense is rank, but he cannot pray. Fully aware of the depth of his guilt, he is unable to respond in cue. So too, Hamlet, with his greater susceptibility, is always in vain attempting to meet his cue. Claudius, like Hamlet, but for opposite reasons, stands in pause, unmoved by the sensitivity that makes Hamlet's life so erratic and subject to the impulses of the instant. Claudius sanely acknowledges that he cannot truly repent while he still has his crown, his ambition, his queen. He realizes that he should be horrified, but cannot respond even when he goes through the act of bending in prayer: "Yet what can it when one cannot repent?" By a delayed reaction that resembles Hamlet's, Claudius seems more moved later, after Polonius has been killed, when he says, "O, come away! My soul is full of discord and dismay."

Polonius also plots in petty ways, but the Polonius time scheme is a different range of horizontality. His only wisdom is the platitude, and the platitude is a mechanical habit. Polonius mouths, and his morality is merely a set of axioms on which he relies but which he hardly believes. Polonius is the conventional moralist, and his own sort of moral paralysis is perfectly indicated in his famous advice to Laertes about being true to himself. The superficiality of this advice is apparent in the pseudo-logic that makes night follow day, not day follow night, as the tenor of the speech would require.

The platitude is a special problem in *Hamlet,* for in a sense everyone speaks platitudes, and it requires discrimination to detect when a platitude is a platitude. The answer is probably that it depends on who is speaking. As Walter Raleigh once said, there are two sorts of platitudes: one that means something to the speaker, and one that means nothing but words. Take three successive speeches in *Hamlet.* First Polonius:

> . . . We are oft to blame in this,
> 'Tis too much proved, that with devotion's visage
> And pious action we do sugar o'er
> The devil himself (III,1)

Then Claudius:

> O 'tis too true . . .
> The harlot's cheek, beautied with plast'ring art,
> Is not more ugly to the thing that helps it
> Than is my deed to my most painted word. . . . (III, 1)

Then Hamlet himself, "To be, or not to be—that is the question," a meditation dangerously in key with the preceding generalities, but saved from being cliché only because Hamlet gives inward meaning to his utterance. Is the same true of Gertrude when, after the closet scene, she too mouths a platitude:

> So full of artless jealousy is guilt
> It spills itself in fearing to be spilt. (IV, 5)

Polonius is not only platitudinous, he repeats. The three most repetitive characters in Shakespeare probably are Pandarus in *Troilus and Cressida*, Polonius, and Hamlet himself, who can seldom say anything once. This repetitiousness indicates some mental blockage or paralysis, and is also a sign of need to give coherence to time, to bind experience by a cyclic or closed boundary from which there is no exit. To command life by the reiterated maxim is a mark of insensitivity or of an incapacity to meet the demands of the vertical instant. To rely on the maxim is to dull the mind to the originality of each moment. The platitude is a vehicle for imposing a superficial order on experience, forcing the unique present minute into a pattern of undiscriminating belief. Obviously Polonius relies upon the platitudes he speaks. Obviously Hamlet, though he speaks platitudes, is troubled by the implications of his own platitudes, some of which are the academic formulas he has begun to suspect. Yet he cannot always free himself from these academisms. When he has seen his father's ghost, he cries for his tables to set down that one may smile and smile and be a villain: "So uncle, there you are"—a reassuring note as if taken from some lecture on life. Usually Hamlet phrases his platitudes in a context of searching doubt, pressed beyond the margin of security. Around Hamlet's maxims are intimations beyond his reach.

Another term for the habitual or stereotyped response would be orthodoxy, the conventionality to which

Polonius is bound. Conventional morality gives horizontal coherence, ossifying itself in words. The maxim is the Maginot Line of the moral life. Since he cannot reconcile or control his responses, Hamlet is extraordinarily aware of the importance of habit. Indeed, the theme of habit or custom is central in the play. Maynard Mack has indicated how there is an association in *Hamlet* between "seeming" and the many images of clothes and habituation. Custom or habit becomes a resource of a Prince lost amid the unrelated crises of his moments. He feels the force of the comment (by Imogen) in *Cymbeline:* "the breach of custom is breach of all." (IV, 2) Everywhere Hamlet discovers breaches of custom, whether in the murder of his father, the adultery of his mother, the infidelity of Ophelia, or betrayals by Rosencrantz and Guildenstern.

It seems legitimate to think that the word *custom* was pronounced with a pun on *costume* or *habit.* If evidence is needed, there is the episode in *The Taming of the Shrew* when Petruchio mocks the gown the Tailor has made for Katherine and dismisses him contemptuously:

> Go, hop me over every kennel home,
> For you shall hop without my custom, sir,
> I'll none of it. (IV, 3)

Custom:costume:habit—habit in at least two senses, the garments one wears and the habits one has. Basic images in this play cluster about disease, rottenness, sexuality, but equally significant are the clothes-habit-costume-custom images, which are astonishingly numerous. To cite a few almost at random: Hamlet's customary suit of black, his trappings of woe, Polonius's reference to Hamlet's vows as bawds invested in dishonest dyes, Polonius's advice about costly apparel, the custom of exercise, the sables of age or the devil, the damned custom that brazens Gertrude's heart, the customs honored in the breach, the custom of easiness in the gravedigger, the good spirits clothing

Horatio, Hamlet's complying with the garb of welcome to
Rosencrantz and Guildenstern, the nighted color (or
choler) of Hamlet's thought, his antic disposition put on,
the glass of fashion, the habit o'erleavening the form of
plausive manners. There are many others.

The profound relation between custom or habit and
Hamlet's desperate need to give coherence—horizontality
—to time involves one of the traditional disciplines in the
moral life. Aristotle's *Ethics* stresses the imperative need
for habit in attaining moral virtue; we become what we
do, he tells us, for the virtues, which are not in us by
nature, can be developed only by habit—by doing the
right thing again and again until we become good
through a moral behaviorism, a conditioned response cul-
tivated by repeated acts that are chosen at first, then performed habitually until they become our nature. Medieval
moralists like Aquinas reemphasized the necessity of *habi-
tus* as spiritual discipline. The monastic life was a recur-
rence of pious acts in ritual form. Thus Aristotle and
Aquinas look upon the good life as a sort of moral drama
—a continual reenactment in performing a role that can
establish virtue. Morality is a chosen automatism that is at
first a seeming, then a reality.

The most significant clothes:habit:custom image occurs
in Hamlet's advice to Gertrude in the closet scene. Hamlet
urges upon his mother the custom that will help bind time
horizontally and give coherence to her life; her repeated
acting of a role will change her nature:

> . . . go not to my uncle's bed.
> Assume a virtue if you have it not.
> That monster custom, who all sense doth eat
> Of habits evil, is angel yet in this,
> That to the use of actions fair and good
> He likewise gives a frock or livery
> That aptly is put on. (III, 4)

Habit and orthodoxy as mere platitudes, habit and orthodoxy as instruments for inducing a sound moral life, the possibility of giving continuity to the time that is out of joint, the mastery of time by custom—all these are inherent in Hamlet's counsel. He is pressing upon his mother a theme that he instinctively knows could bear upon his own life and could bring direction and stability into his own fragmented experience, which is disastrously vertical and subject to the impact of casual impulse.

Since Hamlet's aesthetic sense is as compelling as his moral sense, he attempts to give coherence to his life by playing roles, none of which he can enact convincingly enough to suit his fastidious sensibility. Hamlet's compulsion to play the role well and his troublesome scepticism about all role-playing must reflect Shakespeare's own ostensible doubts about the validity of drama, doubts which cause him repeatedly to remind his audience that the theatre is a mere mockery of "true things" (witness the prologue to Act IV of *Henry V*). "Seems, madam?" says Hamlet, "Nay, it is. I know not 'seems.'" Yet Hamlet is driven by his vivid dramatic imagination to play the revenger's role effectively, and is always doubtful whether he is meeting his cue adequately, or whether he is able to meet his cue at all. That is why Fortinbras torments him. One tell-tale episode is Hamlet's failure to kill Claudius while he prays. Hamlet might do it now, but then Claudius would go to heaven, and the act would be out of the revenger's character. So his sword must know a more horrid hent in a scene where Claudius dies melodramatically in the luxury of his bed. In the same vein Hamlet knows that he cannot play the lover's role, or even the madman's, for he is "ill at these numbers."

His need for consistency in role appears in the closet scene when the ghost urges him to act. Hamlet is again aware that he is not meeting his cue, and begs his father not to look upon him so movingly:

Lest with this piteous action, you convert
My stern effects. Then what I have to do
Will want true colour, tears perchance for blood. (III, 4)

The pun colour-choler proves that Hamlet is still trying to
see himself performing his role in character, which requires him to kill in wrath, not pity. Hamlet's dramatic
view of life—his vision of his role as fatting kites with
Claudius—demands that he give his performance suitable
coherence, which he never can muster, not only because of
his intelligence but also because he is capable of playing
many conflicting roles concurrently, and because his impulses keep breaking in to disrupt the horizontal integrity
of his posturing.

For one thing, there are nearly insoluble problems in
Hamlet's most obvious role-playing. He can sanely and
competently advise the players about acting, warning them
about "inexplicable dumb shows and noise," and begetting
temperance that forbids them to saw the air. But when
Hamlet appears before Ophelia distraught, he seems to
have put on a very bad act indeed of precisely the sort he
has warned against. It would appear to be a travesty of his
own counsel. Is he overacting because he knows that Ophelia is stupid? Is he carried beyond his role by the anguish
of the moment and really mad? At any rate, this performance is a strange one for anybody as finicking as Hamlet
about propriety, especially when he is so irked by the
"damnable faces" of the players enacting the Mouse Trap.

For another thing, his dramatic vision of life does not
seem to cohere because of anachronisms and the discontinuities in time. It is inconceivable to him that Gertrude,
having known his father, could decline upon Claudius,
from Hyperion to a satyr, from wedded fidelity to the rank
garbage of incestuous sheets. The past seems to have no
relation to the present. "Look here upon this picture, and
on this," he tells Gertrude. Before the counterposition of

these two images, logic collapses; the descent is too steep, and Gertrude's character becomes unintelligible. The time is out of joint when lust can mutine in a matron's bones, and frost burns flamingly. Nothing has any relation to the foregoing or succeeding, and the spectacle violates the modesty of nature, failing to show virtue its own image and the time its true form and pressure.

Besides, Hamlet's absurd effort to give dramatic coherence to life brings him into tormented awareness that drama is not life, and he suffers a conflict between his theatrical and his moral impulses. When he hears the player speak his passionate speech about Hecuba, he detects that his aestheticism is not enough. The player breaks through the barrier between acting and living, his dream of passion causing him to weep. Yet Hamlet is so enraptured by theatre that he hopes to snare the conscience of Claudius (Claudius!) by a merely theatrical enactment that will cause him to confess openly. Hamlet's exquisite aestheticism has led him to make a mistake of incredible stupidity, for he presumes that Claudius, too, is gifted with an acute dramatic sensitivity. Never was Hamlet more naive than when he seems to believe that "by the very cunning of the scene" guilty creatures have been so struck to the soul as to proclaim their malefactions. How preposterous to suppose that Claudius, the supremely poised strategist, sane as he is and lacking in refinement, will be touched to the soul. As it turns out, Claudius is duly alarmed but morally invulnerable; he simply contrives to send Hamlet abroad.

The moral involvements for Claudius come, as they do for Hamlet, in arrears, and in the following prayer scene Claudius puts on his own act, going through the motions of repentance, yet knowing all the while—again with immovable sanity—that he should feel guilt, but does not and cannot.[2] The whole scene is a fine counterpoint to the Hamlet player scene when the Hecuba speech breaks down

the player and Hamlet. Hamlet is so moved that he cannot
isolate his dramatic from his moral sense, and he is forced
to recognize the yawning gulf between the role he might
play and his defection from this role. Hamlet goes through
a crisis of conscience, exhibiting the disrelationship between the aesthetic and the ethical. He suffers from this
disrelationship as Claudius cannot. However, Claudius
suffers his own kind of paralysis. He performs his own
dramatic act, but is unmoved by this act. Hamlet is capable
of being carried away by the role he plays. Claudius, with
his undeviating sense of reality, sees himself praying but
knows that he is not penitent. His conscience is not caught
by the theatrical gesture. As he kneels, he realizes that his
performance is an empty one, since he wills to keep his
crown and his queen. It is a mere rehearsal for an act of
repentance.

In contrast with Claudius's paralysis, in which the dramatic gesture does not work, there immediately follows the
closet scene when Hamlet admonishes his mother to put on
a morally effective act by staying out of his uncle's bed, that
is, to put on the frock or livery of good custom. Here, he
hopes, the dramatic role will secure a moral reformation
that will "change the stamp of nature."

In thus advising Gertrude, Hamlet passes beyond the
fine aestheticism of his advice to the players, urging them
to play their roles with temperance and propriety. In
speaking to the players, he seems to feel that by suiting the
word and gesture to the act, the actor can endow nature
with modesty, intelligibility, and coherence that life itself
lacks. But this is, at its best, only regulating life by aesthetic
measure. In his sermon to Gertrude the aestheticism is
gone; a moral regeneration is thought to emerge from an
enacted role. In admonishing his mother, Hamlet supposes
that by meeting her cues properly she can insure her moral
condition. In this deeper moral enactment she is not *cast*
into the role she plays; she must assume responsibility for
choosing her role. The moral act must be elected.

Then it must be repeated, lending an easiness to the next abstinence. Thus there is a difference between the repetitiveness of a Polonius (whose morality is a *bad* act, not consciously willed) and the repetitiveness Hamlet recommends on Aristotelian grounds, the habitual or ritual cultivation of virtue by continually performing an act that is determinedly put on.

One of the perennial and stubborn questions in criticism has been the relation between art and life. The heart of Hamlet's mystery is here involved. In the closet scene—which is at odds with the preceding prayer scene with Claudius—Hamlet gives answer to the art-life dilemma: dramatic role-playing can have effects on the way we live. The repeated acting of a chosen role can give direction and stability to the self seeking virtue. After his malign and cunning theatrical exploit in arranging the Mouse Trap playlet to catch Claudius's conscience, Hamlet suddenly finds a key to life in moral behaviorism. Habit becomes character; the role becomes reality.

In sum, Hamlet rejects one behaviorism for another. The earlier behaviorism of his antic disposition, his frantic jesting, his overresponses was a nearly automatic succession of reflexes that revealed the extreme disorientation of Renaissance man and the same mobility of attention we find in Leonardo. Hamlet's life was a breach of custom, and his unstable reactions might be explained by William James's remark that we need habit because we are born with a tendency to do more things than our nerve centers can arrange naturally to do. So Hamlet attempted to give order and direction to his incoherent responses by translating them into a dramatic action in which he might play a role "in character." Along with this dramatic venture Hamlet made an equally strenuous effort to plot his way out of his disorientation. Both attempts failed since both were a false mastery of time; his experience still disintegrated under him. Then in dealing with his mother's moral plight, he invoked habit as a moral discipline, a control of time that begins with an act chosen for the moment *(pro tem)* but strengthens by repetition into a virtue that gives ethical continuity to behavior.

When the act is automatic, not chosen, we descend to the behaviorsim of Polonius, who lacks the integrity arising from self-awareness, self-scrutiny, and moral purpose. Lacking this purpose, the enactment of a role can be corrupted. Polonius stupidly belies his own plea for integrity by his sordid plotting, the deviousness that makes his precaution a false wisdom and his conduct a fraudulence:

> And thus do we of wisdom, and of reach,
> With windlasses and with assays of bias,
> By indirections find directions out. (II, 1)

This is dishonest drama, mere appearance.

Polonius's plotting is evidence of his bad faith. His suspicion leads him to a desire for proof, the proof that is needed when one distrusts, when one cannot believe, even in one's own son. Hamlet too seeks proof, but with his prophetic soul Hamlet is not really concerned with proof. When he has the evidence of Claudius's crime as a result of the playlet, he does not act upon it. Hamlet is always seeking something more sustaining than proof; he quests for honesty, for good faith, which he requires from Ophelia, from Rosencrantz and Guildenstern, and which he finds only in Horatio. The desire for proof, like the tactic of plotting, is a perversion of the intellect in its attempt to give life and time a false coherence and logic.

The stability of life must arise from trust, belief, good faith, all wanting in Denmark. The devious wisdom of Polonius, a correlate of his dishonesty, suspicion, and lack of integrity, is sign of the corruption that makes everyone in Denmark an opportunist. Polonius is eager to exploit the chance to wed his daughter well. Here again we have a complication in the time scheme of the play, for Polonius, Claudius, Fortinbras, and Hamlet himself all improvise.

Improvisation springs from the opportunities of the moment: Fortinbras finds quarrel in a straw; Polonius rushes to the king with the news that his daughter had a letter; Hamlet leaves his mother's chamber, having killed Polonius on the instant, with the clever plan of hoisting Claudius with his own petard:

> . . . O, 'tis most sweet
> When in one line two crafts directly meet.

Improvising differs from plotting in that the continuity of time is required for plotting, but not for improvising, where there is a reliance on the creative possibilities of the instant. Hamlet's plotting usually has the air of improvising, and his improvising is often vicious, as when he forges the document that sends Rosencrantz and Guildenstern to their death. His brain began the play before the prologue; the deception is nearly unconsidered. And when Horatio is uneasy about this viciousness, Hamlet shows himself to be quite callous—as callous as Claudius, in fact. They are not near his conscience but simply fall between the incensed points of mighty opposites. In *Hamlet*, therefore, the plotting often disintegrates into the *ad hoc* treacheries offered by the moment.

Improvising is one way of submitting to the verticality of time, making the present work. The present works for Fortinbras and for Claudius, but not, at first, for Hamlet. The present begins to work for Hamlet when, during the pirate attack, he boards the vessel in the grapple. Hamlet's letter recounting this event is puzzling, for he says that the pirates dealt with him like thieves of mercy, knowing what they did. Is it possible that Hamlet had prearranged this attack? If so, Hamlet has at last engineered a successful plot. Yet even if it is only improvising, an irony enters, since Claudius had supposed that sending Hamlet abroad would expel the poisons in him. Claudius did not realize that Hamlet would in fact return after the pirate episode with the poison somehow expelled. Hamlet lands naked, as the Dane, apparently having worked off his paralysis either in the malignly improvised trick for killing Rosencrantz and Guildenstern or else having realized his ability to act by leaping aboard the pirate craft.

The turning point in the time scheme of the play occurs when Hamlet, having put his plotting behind him, lands in Denmark receptive to a new mode of improvising, or yielding to time instead of trying to control it. In the fifth act, which opens in the graveyard, Hamlet learns the most valuable of all his lessons, revising his Wittenberg education, namely, that one must humble himself before time, that one cannot engineer its course, and that the present is more real than a future controlled by plotting or by any logic to master the outcome of events.[3] Time is not, then, governed by purpose, least of all by criminal purpose. Hamlet learns to improvise in a quite different mode; one must submit to the present occasion, or what time brings. And time brings death.

This humility before the present could be called drifting, since Hamlet appears to drift to his death and, incidentally, to the solution of all his problems. But it is not exactly drifting, or not drifting as Polonius drifted. Hamlet's loss of direction is, and is not, like Polonius's loss of direction. Polonius, like Hamlet early in the play, suffers from inconclusiveness, losing his way amid his intricate assays of bias: "What was I about to say? By the mass, I was about to say something." There is some similarity between Hamlet's indecisions, his evasions, his hesitations and misgivings, and the devious or muddled course of Polonius, who thinks he can command events by his machinations, his spying, his deductions. Both Polonius and Hamlet lose direction within the confines of their own devices and thus sterilize the present.

At the close, however, Hamlet drifts otherwise, accepting the sufficiency of the present moment without trying to manipulate it for his own purpose. This new sense of the verticality of time—a reception of what happens as it happens—enables him to act, to validate the moment at hand. The gravedigger, convincing him of the base uses to which we all return, faces Hamlet with the ultimate boundary of time, beyond which time ceases to have meaning. The absurdity of death, making dust of the conqueror of history, and of time, has been in the background of Hamlet's mind since the beginning. Time now seems to Hamlet to have a benignity, since the houses a gravedigger makes last until doomsday. With this new sense of fatality Hamlet is able to surrender his plotting, his ingenious games of hoisting the engineer with his own petard. He is able to act on the faith that the readiness is all. The present occasion is adequate, and he acquiesces to the present moment (the vertical) without anxiety for the future.

The religious phrase to designate Hamlet's final submission to time would be acceptance of providence. On shipboard Hamlet evidently came to realize how impossible it is to control one's fate; thus he begins to trust the occasion even though he feels a kind of fighting in his heart. The impromptu act becomes a form of resignation. He tells Horatio that our indiscretions serve us well when plots begin to pall; we must learn that a divinity shapes our ends. Hamlet is now fully conscious of the very principle he himself had written into the playlet in which he hoped to catch Claudius's conscience:

> Our wills and fates do so contrary run
> That our devices still are overthrown;
> Our thoughts are ours, their ends none of our own. (III, 2)

So against the graveyard experience Hamlet is willing to accept the invitation to duel; his purpose will follow the king's pleasure: "If his fitness speaks, mine is ready; now or whensoever." Then for the first time in the play, Horatio, the man of good faith, advises strategy, offering to forestall the duel. But Hamlet will have no more plotting. Turning from his earlier devices, Hamlet replies in words that summarize what he never learned at Wittenberg, words almost Biblical:

> There is a special providence in the fall of a sparrow. If it be now, 'tis not to come; if it be not to come, it will be now; if it be not now, yet it will come. The readiness is all. . . . Let be. (V, 2)

Hamlet the intellectual and Borgia has yielded to Hamlet the man of good faith. The bad dreams are gone, and he knows that the plotting and role-playing are done. His former life was an evasion or shuffling. The term *shuffling* is singularly prominent in *Hamlet* (*scuffling* has the same root). Hamlet senses that in the world beyond the whips and scorns of time there is no shuffling. Claudius surprisingly in his prayer scene repeats that "above" there is no shuffling, and later he advises Laertes that with a little shuffling (scuffling) the rapiers can be exchanged. At the last Hamlet in his scuffling with Laertes puts off his previous shuffling, making the present work for him.

In the duel with Laertes the fissure between the theatrical and the moral act finally closes. Hamlet dies in an act of play, in a new dramatic episode where he absurdly assumes a modish or dandiacal role. Claudius is never shrewder than when he realizes how Hamlet will be stung by Lamord's praise of Laertes as a duelist. Hamlet goes to death ridiculously in a fashionable exercise played on the spur of the moment, where nothing is at stake but *succès d'estime*. Hamlet dies to maintain his image in the glass of fashion, but in playing this genteel game he resolves his deepest problems. That is the irony. When he goes to duel Laertes—seizing the moment *ad hoc* upon the request of Osric, his foppish alter ego—Hamlet is not only a man of mode; he is a scapegoat, a victim, a sacrifice to the rotten state of Denmark. He perishes as an innocent. Hamlet's foregoing games were mostly cynical. His final game is played in trust, humility, submission to others and to the given moment.

The difference between the final Hamlet and the earlier Hamlet can be measured by the cynicism of his great speech about Fortinbras's political game, for Fortinbras is playing the game of honor Hamlet feels impelled to play, and cannot. Hamlet the intellectual, the prince who here is as sane as Claudius, perceives that to play this game of power politics one must find his quarrel in a mere straw— a quarrel that can only lead to an imposthume in the state, and a conquest so empty that the gained ground will not suffice to bury the slain. This cynicism is necessary, even wholesome, and Hamlet's worldly wisdom is never more cogent than in rejecting the Fortinbras romanticism. Fortinbras is a mad opportunist.

Hamlet's opportunism in dueling is neither drifting nor strategy. It is an impromptu act that makes time poetic in Bachelard's sense of the term, the momentary decision that bears the mark of originality in life, the instant that emerges within a framework of discontinuity, the accident that is creative. Hamlet achieves his revenger's purpose and meets his fate in a moment that fulfils the possibilities of time in an act of play: Osric, angel of death, comes in guise of a coxcomb.

That Hamlet should die in a game is a strange mastery of time. Roger Caillois has written that play reduces life to certain rules, to a ritual activity performed in an *as if* context, as if the game were reality. This *as if* context is the link between drama and play. Among the categories of the game is *alea*, the chance that counterfeits reality, the drawing of lots or the *sortes* that are a guise of fatality. In games of *alea* the necessary, the logical, the foreseen, the predictive yield to hazard, and the player submits to a situation that corresponds religiously to providence. The extreme of providence is the Calvinist belief that only God knows and

decides. The chance over which we have no control but to
which we submit, that is the game Hamlet is at last willing
to play when he duels. He predicts, to be sure, that he will
win at the odds since he has been in practice. But over
against his assurance is his new resignation to the occasion:
"Let be." He is willing to allow divinity to shape the end,
to watch the contingent emerge.

Games of *alea* impinge on the sacred for, as Caillois remarks, the sacred is a world of danger where there are
forces man cannot control. These forces are symbolized by
the throw of the dice, which is the poetry of vertical time.
Bachelard says that a poem validates an instant, occurring
in vertical time because it negates all past and future experience and stands out in its own integrity and surprise. The
poem is the fruition inherent in the present moment, and
there is always something impromptu in the poem as an
emergence from the occasion *hic et nunc*, here and now, a
revelation that was unforeseen, unexpected, and fully re-
ceived in its possibilities and ambiguities.

Another irony is that Claudius, who has tried to master
time by crime, by strategy, by provisions against surprise,
should suddenly come to his death precisely at that moment when he has plotted Hamlet's death by the double
means of rapier and poison. At the end Claudius, like Hamlet, discovers the validity of the present, which cannot be
engineered. The anachronisms in *Hamlet* are often due to
that perversion of the intellect that would regulate time by
prearrangement, plotting, attempting to secure the future
instead of acceding to the present in its uncertainty and
promise. Hamlet the intellectual, the aesthete, the moralist
learns that one does not conquer time except by yielding
to the creative value in the passing moment.

Hamlet faces the same obligation as Hal—to redeem the
time. And Hamlet, like Hal, redeems the time by finding
that only through time is time conquered. Hal ceases to
evade time when he abandons his pleasures in Eastcheap

and assumes the duty of kingship, embarking on his imperialist venture abroad. Hal's evasions are finally put behind
him the night before Agincourt when, face to face with
Williams the ordinary soldier, he copes with the responsibility of the regent who leads his men into dubious battle,
a responsibility Fortinbras never had a chance to examine,
though Hamlet pondered it. In Hamlet's case the dubiety
is not political but personal, yet the conclusion seems to be
the same, namely, that the present in its uncertainty is the
ground for assurance, authenticity, and freedom.

From Bachelard's point of view the meaning of *Hamlet*
is that discontinuous or punctiform time is the source of
creative existence, and that the venture of giving life coherence by mind or art is destined to fail. Neither time,
thought nor the aesthetic sense can give life unity. The
time in *Hamlet* is out of joint; but tempo, not time, is deci-
sive. The constant fluctuation in pace, scene after scene,
gives this play its own dramatic calibre: from fury to meditation, from haste to pause, from anguish to poise, from
cynicism to raging idealism, from frantic jesting to calcula-
tion, from sneaking suspicion to honesty—the modulation
of a temperament that lives in the instant but, until the end,
refuses the instant. Until then, Hamlet's efforts to give
continuity and intelligibility to time lead only to baffle-
ment, frustration, disillusion, and the delay that is defection and defeat. When he begins to improvise, taking the
moment as it comes, he no longer suffers the whips and
scorns of time. He finds that fulfillment and freedom arise
not by designing the future or even understanding the past,
but, instead, by conceding to the surprising possibilities
that open from the present.

V

Duration: Macbeth

It is a sign of Shakespeare's receptivity to different modes of human experience that *Hamlet* is a play committed to the crises of discontinuous instants whereas *Macbeth* is a play fusing time into Bergsonian duration, a time sense in which instants are absorbed into a state of consciousness that is like a continuum. In each play time is out of joint, yet the anachronism in *Hamlet* is not the anachronism in *Macbeth*. In contrast to Hamlet's punctual time sense, Macbeth's time sense is an ellipsis or condensation of past, present, and future that might be called synoptic montage.[1] The two plays represent two kinds of fatality—the fatality of the contingent and the fatality of the necessary. And behind the two differing anachronisms are different conceptions of freedom. *Hamlet* has the freedom of the vertical instant, which is genetic, an opportunism opening the full possibilities inherent in the unexpected and accepted moment. *Macbeth* has the other kind of freedom implied in the Greek proverb that a man's character is his fate, as if by chosen self-realization. The play is a study in the moral life that is "destined" in Bergson's sense of the term.

Durative time is the tragic time that is a stasis, as in the action of *Oedipus the King*, which is simply an occasion leading him to recognize that his misfortune was predetermined by his nature. This tragic view is retrospective or, it might be said, demonstrative of what should have been apparent sooner. Hence tragic irony, the gap that opens between what might have been and what is done. For Oedipus and for Macbeth the outcome was already there in their natures before it occurred.

Bergson has been attacked for the imprecisions and perhaps the confusions in his thought, but books like *Time and Free Will, Creative Evolution,* and *The Two Sources of Morality and Religion* have many passages bearing on the anachronisms that link *Macbeth* with the Sophoclean tragedy. Throughout, Bergson insists upon the difference between time as lived and time as thought. That is, he contrasts durative or psychic time with serial or chronometric time, the time rationalized into successive periods by the clock or calendar. As intuitionist and vitalist Bergson distrusts the intellect as an instrument for comprehending the moral life, since this life has rhythms that cannot be measured in quantitative units. The moral life has a continuity and direction unintelligible to reason; the temporal intervals progressing on the clock are for Bergson only a device for parceling time into a scheme of past, present, and future—then, now, or to come. Thus to divide time into sequential phases is to falsify the psychic life by fragmenting it. To conceive the moral life, or consciousness, in a series of identifiable timespans is to fraction existence into periods that are at best only abstractions. These periods are relevant to time in the external world. As Anton Ehrenzweig has written, "The illusion of temporal sequence is perhaps the most cogent of all externality illusions; . . . and this mode is externalized into the outer world and perceived there as an objective order in time which all natural events have to follow."

An extreme form of fragmenting time into rational units was the Newtonian world order in which the flow of absolute time could be broken down into episodes isolated within the here and now. Whitehead has mentioned how this mechanical view was an invention of the 17th century, the century of mathematical genius. Under the Newtonian regime the world seemed to be "a succession of instantaneous configurations" here in space and then in time. Whitehead terms such designation a fallacy of simple location, since every event can be thought to occur at a certain place at a certain time "apart from any essential reference of the relations . . . to other regions of space and to other durations of time." As was suggested in the first chapter, this Newtonian mechanism pertains to what Heidegger calls the *Umwelt*, the world of things in nature. Other worlds, the *Mitwelt* and the *Eigenwelt*, the social and psychic worlds of moral and tragic life, cannot be known by the temporal scheme we impose upon events in the *Umwelt*. Particularly in the *Eigenwelt* experience is anachronistic, reflexive, and vibratory.

A number of Bergson's statements enable us to characterize the durative time of consciousness. In the flow of psychic life the past prolongs itself into the present, and the present has within itself intimations of the future, a foreknowledge that brings inquietude. Within the fusions of psychic time (which is moral time) "we feel the different parts of our being enter into each other, and our whole personality concentrate itself in a point, or rather a sharp edge, pressed against the future and cutting into it unceasingly." Under psychic pressures, "it is with our entire past, including the original bent of our soul, that we desire, will and act." The tragic act is a summation of what we were, are, and will be; it is synoptic. The seemingly discontinuous intervals of the psychic life have antecedents and projections that testify to the endurance of the self. Oedipus was blind before he blinded himself. Macbeth was a bloody man before he murdered Duncan or performed the act that expressed his moral being. The tragic act has behind it, within it, a totality of existence, even if we drag our past behind us unaware. The moral life at its freest and fullest is anachronistic.

Bergson is offended by the intellectualist fallacy he calls finalism, the positing of an end toward which we confidently move, an attraction toward a known or envisioned future he finds delusory. Finalism is a form of mechanism to extract from the ambiguity of our evolution a rational goal to which we can proceed methodically. As vitalist Bergson distrusts any such rational clarification of the flow of being, for our evolution is a ripening, not an engineering, of action. The mind can conceive an end toward which activity is directed, the point of rest toward which to move, but it cannot comprehend the obscurities or uncertainties inherent in the very moving toward that end: "the movements constituting the action itself either elude our consciousness or reach it only confusedly." In the simple act of raising the arm, we cannot imagine beforehand the complexity of the contractions and tensions involved in the intended elevation. If any act "involves the whole person and is truly ours," the obscurities thicken until "our conduct slips between" our rational notions. Since the tragic act is a synopsis of our being, it is surrounded by a "fringe of darkness" fading off into experiences the mind does not penetrate: "The intellect is characterized by a natural inability to comprehend life."

Thus Bergson assumes that man is in an absurd position when he rationalizes his life, for the intellect phrases problems it cannot solve except through the grid of logic. If our evolution occurs in psychic time, it must be lived, not thought. When time is thought, it is spatialized, split into successive moments, yet when we live, we cannot isolate our present from our former states of consciousness. "Pure duration is the form which the succession of our conscious states assumes when our ego lets itself *live*, when it refrains from separating its present state from its former states." In durative time, says Bergson, moments "permeate each other" like colors on the neck of a dove. Time becomes "iridescent." Our deep states of consciousness have no relation to quantity; "they are pure quality," the whole person being immersed in a psychic atmosphere. Our lived time goes by intensities, not logic. At this height of consciousness, "there is no difference between foreseeing, seeing, and acting."

Much of what Bergson says about duration in psychic experience rephrases the situation in Athenian tragedy dealing so obscurely with the choices before man. In Aeschylus's *Suppliants*, King Pelasgus, facing the decision whether to give refuge to Danaus's daughters, exclaims, "The choices are hard. The issue is dark." One does not make such choices by reason but by intuition. Throughout Greek drama, especially in Sophocles and Euripides, the mind does not help. Jocasta, the intelligent woman, knows that oracles are undependable, but she suffers none the less. Oedipus attempts to circumvent the oracle, and his attempt brings only the inevitable recognition of his own nature. Euripides as rationalist suspects the gods, but he knows that the gods merit piety even if they behave ineligibly. The oracles speak truth after all.

Like some Euripidean intellectual, Hamlet discovers that there are thoughts beyond the reaches of his soul. Hamlet, however, unlike Macbeth, is a modern man, born of a new Renaissance sense of individuality, a consciousness of his need for identity. Identity is not a question for Macbeth. From the first Macbeth knows who he is, but he refuses that knowledge. Like Oedipus, Macbeth has his identity, which he must be driven to recognize. Macbeth has a strong character but not the complex individuality of a Hamlet. Hamlet's individuality is an aspect of his neuroses, which in turn are symptomatic of a diffusion of personality, a negative identity that changes according to the situations he faces and the many roles he is capable of playing. By contrast, Macbeth has a character that is constant, an evil man with an acute moral sensitivity. It is almost futile to ask who is the real Hamlet. Macbeth was always what he intuited himself to be, a bloody man.

Macbeth suffers a division within his own nature and exactly fits the definition of a tragic character offered by Robert B. Heilman in *Tragedy and Melodrama.* Heilman argues that tragedy requires a conflict of imperatives within the self, a conflict driving this character to a moral choice. Macbeth had a double nature, gripped as it was between his moral and criminal imperatives, and under the prompting of Lady Macbeth, he chooses to obey the criminal imperative. This psychic situation is simpler than that in Hamlet, who has not only imperatives but also what Heilman calls impulses, the onset of transitory desires, wishes, inclinations that have no constants behind them. Impulses have no necessary relation to the moral life; imperatives do. Macbeth suffers the division of his double nature. Hamlet suffers not only this division of imperatives; he exists in a state of confusion because of his erratic, momentary impulses, which are unpolarized. Macbeth's imperatives are reduced to an almost epic conflict of duties.

This difference in character may partially account for the difference in time schemes in the two plays, the Hamlet time scheme pivoting on discontinuous instants in all their disrelationships, the Macbeth time scheme static much as the time scheme in *Oedipus* is static, for the action in Sophocles is simply a revelation of what already existed before the action began. The revelation in *Hamlet* is not the revelation in *Macbeth* or *Oedipus.* At the very start of the play Oedipus is inside the labyrinth, though he either does not know it or refuses to recognize it. The play is really his discovery or recognition that he is where he is, and why. Thus too at the start Macbeth is inside the labyrinth—the labyrinth of his own nature. The murder, whose thought is yet fantastic, shakes his state as if it were already done.

In any event, the difference between the revelation in *Hamlet* and revelation in *Macbeth* or *Oedipus* illustrates the distinction between narrative and plot *(mythos)* as Aristotle conceives it. At the close of *Hamlet* there is a revelation of the necessity of accepting the contingent, and the whole action is an exploration of critical instants, each leading, surprisingly and unpredictably, in its own direction. In *Macbeth* and *Oedipus* there is plot in the Aristotelian sense; the terms of action are all given so that Macbeth or Oedipus has only to experience the transformation of first surmises to horrid actualities. Macbeth might say with Eliot: "In my beginning is my end." *Hamlet* is an open action; *Macbeth* is closed.

The closure in *Macbeth* has a curious effect on irony in this play, which is unlike the classic irony in *Oedipus*. When at the start of the Sophoclean drama Oedipus announces that there is a foul thing in Thebes to be expelled, he does not understand the meaning of his words, though he speaks better than he knows (we can hardly believe, as Vellacott suggests, that Oedipus knows the extent of his guilt).[2] This classic irony arises from the ignorance of the speaker. But when Macbeth hears the witches, he already intuits the truth he refuses to phrase except obliquely: the frightening suggestion of this supernatural soliciting cannot be either good or ill, though it unfixes his hair, shaking him to distraction. Macbeth has prescience of what he will do, why he will do it, what the consequences may be. He is his own oracle and eiron. In *Oedipus* the oracle is more dimly understood, and Tiresias acts the role of eiron, warning of the danger. Banquo, who corresponds to the Tiresias figure, is an ineffectual eiron. The special irony in *Macbeth* is not speaking with good but ignorant intent; it is going the way one already fears to go. Macbeth's experience as a moral being is close to the phenomenon of *déjà vu*, a psychic state in which we seem already to have been through the present moment at an earlier time.

There is irony in Macbeth's double nature in the gap that originally exists between his immoral and moral imperatives, a gap that is closed as the play moves toward total crime, much as the gap of ignorance is closed by increasing knowledge in classic irony. If we take the tragic hero to be greater and better than most men but with a fault in his nature, the question can be raised whether Macbeth is eligible for such heroism. We ask whether Macbeth is better than others, whether he is not a unique figure—a Claudius endowed with conscience. His double nature at last becomes single, prevailingly criminal.

Many have commented on the double language of the play: both worlds; lost and won; cannot be ill, cannot be good; highly and holily; makes, mars; rest, labor; lesser, greater; night, day; purpose, deed; double trust; done double; twice seen; both sides even. This equivocating language also indicates that Macbeth knows where he stands so ambiguously, that there is no tragic blindness. He is among the most morally aware Shakespearian figures.

Yet the play has its own obscurity; it is one of the most nocturnal dramas. Above all others it moves between two worlds, much as Sophoclean drama moved between two worlds, local and supernal. The canons of the supernal worlds were often phrased in the riddling replies of the Greek oracle, and the witches in *Macbeth* can be heard as chthonic voices of immeasurable antiquity like the voices once heard at Delphi or in the sacred grove at Colonus. These voices speak dimly of the future, and Judah Stampfer has remarked how Shakespeare treats time as "the shadowy mysterious organism of events, coextensive with the processes of the entire cosmos." The Elizabethans sensed, like the Greeks, the interpenetration of the microcosm and macrocosm, the interdependence of the provincial and universal order. When the woods close in on Dunsinane, these auguries with their archetypal overtones are fulfilled.

Macbeth, the briefest of the tragedies, has a cosmic perspective, timeless, reaching toward the last syllable of our daily pace. The action takes place in Scotland but extends into the vast realm of all our yesterdays and tomorrows, making our deeds seem nothing. As with Sophocles, the world of *nomos* (the local) is seen against the world of *phusis*, the laws written eternally in the heavens. The morning after Duncan is murdered Ross speaks like someone in Sophocles as he refers to the interdependence of two worlds between which the play moves:

> Thou seest the heavens, as troubled with man's act,
> Threatens his bloody stage. By the clock 'tis day,
> And yet dark night strangles the travelling lamp. (II, 4)

The firmament is stained by Duncan's gore, and at the close Malcolm invokes the sanction of higher laws:

> . . . Macbeth
> Is ripe for shaking, and the powers above
> Put on their instruments. (IV, 3)

In this archetypal tragic world the mandates of the cosmos abide in spite of the sins of men. The tragic world in *Macbeth* is the double order envisioned by Antigone: eternal and temporal. When Macbeth plans Banquo's murder he recklessly defies these eternal laws:

> . . . let the frame of things disjoint, both the worlds suffer,
> Ere we will eat our meal in fear . . . (III, 2)

He is afflicted with the guilt that contaminates the whole of nature, for all the oceans, he feels, cannot cleanse his hand, which incarnadines the seas until they turn one red. His vision is cosmic.

This totality of consciousness has been attributed to the tragic view that is retrospective—as if the protagonist saw things fully by looking backward after the crisis.[3] That is, tragic vision is not so much a representation of events as they happen as it is a reexperiencing of the events as if from a subsequent position, bringing the whole action into synoptic unity. This retrospective view is not merely a flashback but a meditative regard of what happens, detaching the hero from his involvement in the events in which he takes part. This quasi-retrospective recognition is a height of consciousness bringing to tragedy a sense of inevitability, a self-judgment inherent in the action.

Such vision as if from beyond, implicit in tragic apprehension, is anachronistic, available only through a certain emancipation from the serial course of events. The image of the labyrinth is again useful: the protagonist, having this tragic consciousness, perceives how the course of events makes a design, and his perception of this design brings a sense of fatality that is static, total, and timeless. We cannot claim that all tragedy is handled from this retrospective view, yet from the first Macbeth's intimations of his bloody nature endow him with an intuition of the inevitability of his course and induce him to censure himself for his acts even before they are done. Even while he murders Macbeth is aware how (in Eliot's words):

> Time present and time past
> Are both perhaps present in time future,
> And time future contained in time past.

Hamlet lacks this consciousness of the totality of his course, and his commitment to the crisis of the instant blinds him with an ignorance quite unlike Macbeth's awareness of his situation precisely while he is moving through it. Hamlet happens upon his fate; time for him is mobile, a continual innovation, an extension of possibilities. Time comes to Macbeth in another mode, since the future is there before it occurs. His moments permeate each other, and, in Bergson's phrase, there is for him no difference between seeing, foreseeing, and acting. Existing in duration, he cannot separate his present state from his former or future states. His past is coextensive with his present and his future. This montage effect is lacking in Hamlet, who learns a different lesson—the need to let be, to take what the moment can give. Hamlet's career does not make a unity; Macbeth's does. Hamlet's course is developmental; Macbeth's is foreordained by his nature.

During his career Macbeth is in flight from the intuition

that he is what he is: "To know my deed, 'twere best not know myself." In spite of this willed ignorance, his realization is unavoidable. As is true of Oedipus, nothing really happens in this play, for there is only recognition, *anagnorisis,* and the events are the vehicles to enforce this recognition. Macbeth has the classical tragic stasis, the arrest of action into a design predestined.

In no Shakespearean drama—perhaps in no other play— is the tragic anachronistic and durative mode so dominant. Macbeth's moral intuition is so vivid that present, past, and future amalgamate. His experience has total integrity; there is no character development; all is given at the start. Richard Flatter has noted how the ambiguity of language here involves more than double phrasings, for there is an interpenetration of grammatical aspect and mood and tense. Aspect is that feature of tense indicating whether the action is punctual or continuing and iterative: is, do, did vs. am doing, was doing, will be doing. Throughout *Macbeth* there is an almost indiscriminate appearance of punctual with iterative aspect, along with a suggestive fusion of indicative with optative or imperative modes; and the tenses stand side by side in a kind of montage of inflection. This montage reveals how Macbeth cannot distinguish the actual from the imagined, the present from the past, the past from the future:

> *Is* this a dagger which I see before me,
> The handle toward my hand? Come, *let* me clutch thee!
> I *have* thee not, and yet I see thee still. . . .
> Thou marshall'st me the way that I *was* going,
> And such an instrument I *was* to use . . .
> I go, and it *is* done . . . (II, 1)

The present tense carries the import of the retrospective future, a syntactic paradox. Notoriously Macbeth's sense of guilt is phrased in obscure subjunctives, fusing the hypothetical with the actual and accepting the future as the present by a retrospective vision converting what is to be done into what is already done: "If it were done when 'tis done, then 'twere well/ It were done quickly." With oracular foresight Macbeth knows that pity shall blow the deed in every eye until tears drown the wind. His ambition has leaped over itself, and he is already on the far side of time to come. As the play draws to its end, Macbeth is increasingly burdened by the anachronism of his life, which at this advanced hour should have brought him honor, love, obedience, but these have all turned sear instead of accompanying age. The dislocation of time is not, for him, the surprising discontinuity of Hamlet's disjunctive experience; it is a condensation of his whole existence into an enduring disaster that was there from the first.

According to accepted Elizabethan psychology (which confirmed certain moral imperatives) reason should be lord of will and appetite. The proper function of reason is to order experience so that it is not governed by will or passion. In a notable phrase spoken the hour after he murders Duncan, Macbeth mentions "the pauser reason." Macduff asks Macbeth why he so impetuously killed Duncan's grooms. Macbeth replies:

> Who can be wise, amazed, temperate and furious,
> Loyal and neutral, in a moment? No man.
> The expedition of my violent love
> Outrun the pauser reason. (II, 3)

Macbeth is lying, but his specious explanation is in contrast to the implications of Malcolm's speech to Macduff in the great ritual scene when the heir apparent is catechised in a ceremonial act of initiation or testing. Malcolm states that Macbeth has sought to win him over, but "modest wisdom plucks me/ From over-credulous haste." Malcolm obeys the pauser reason. Macbeth is induced by his wife to jump the bank and shoal of time by abandoning the faculty of reason, which should enforce a restraint that can give time—natural, moral, or political time—a due and measured sequence, progress, and succession. The function of reason is to allow time to unfold in proper intervals. In discarding the pauser reason, Macbeth commits himself to tomorrow before today, denying his earlier insight that "Time and the hour runs through the roughest day," resolving what man cannot resolve.

In negating the reason that orders human time Macbeth reaches hell. It is often said that *Macbeth* is a hellish play, that the central symbol in it is the nocturnal scene when the Porter answers the knocking at the gate and identifies Dunsinane with an Inferno. Dante referred to hell as a place where souls have lost the use of reason, and in the Inferno there is an anachronism: the damned know the past and the future, but are blind to the present. Thus the ordering of time is of no value to them, and they exist in a state of ignorance that is felt as despair. Macbeth comes to this same despair.

The temporal montage in *Macbeth* is exactly described when the news comes that Macduff has fled to England and Macbeth realizes that he has lost control of the time he has violated by denying the pauser reason:

> Time, thou anticipat'st my dread exploits.
> The flighty purpose never is o'ertook
> Unless the deed go with it. From this moment
> The very firstlings of my heart shall be
> The firstlings of my hand. And even now,
> To crown my thoughts with acts, be it thought and
>   done. (IV, 1)

As he explains to Lady Macbeth, he has entered the absurdity of a state where action is coincidental with thought, or even precedes thought, and the course of time becomes uncontrolled, directionless:

> . . . I am in blood
> Stepped in so far, that should I wade no more,

> Returning were as tedious as go o'er.
> Strange things I have in head, that will to hand
> Which must be acted ere they may be scanned. (III, 4)

When Macbeth asks Macduff who can be wise, temperate, furious in a moment, one might reply: Hamlet, whose impulses so conflict that they collide at each crisis, paralyzing him. Delay is injurious in *Hamlet;* Macbeth needs to delay. Hamlet lives in time as Macbeth does not, for Hamlet is like Montaigne, fluctuating and *ondoyant.* Macbeth does not fluctuate in this way; he is constantly fighting a rearguard action against the moral imperatives he has stifled and which he negates by the act that precedes or negates thought.

For Hamlet the future is a real and possible value. Macbeth, who has attained his future already, has no career open to him except to accept himself. In *Hamlet* time is discontinuous rather than serial; in *Macbeth* time is monolithic. The Macbeth time montage is apparent in his final deliberated vision: his wife should have died hereafter in the normal course of time; the tomorrows that creep from day to day are indistinguishable from the yesterdays that lighted fools to their death in the past. The stasis is absurd, the idiocy of the bygone being no different from the idiocies to come. Time is beyond the possibility of redemption. The very recognition of this idiocy is proof that Macbeth, passing such judgment, was never able to negate his moral imperatives. His verdict on the meaninglessness of chronological time is an act of the moral imagination.

Lady Macbeth is incapable of such moral verdicts. She lives in a different time scheme, which Bergson would call serial or chronometric. If Macbeth is a criminal endowed with a moral sense, his wife is a criminal *tout court.* She exemplifies Bergson's thesis that the intellect raises problems that it cannot solve. Her ideas are clear and, unlike Macbeth's, do not fade off into a fringe of darkness. She plots, like Claudius, and has a mentality that, later, reappeared in scientific guise in the Newtonian mechanism where time is fragmented into a succession of periods that can be designated as past, present, and future, no one of which impinges on the others. "What's done is done," she tells her husband. The past is isolated in the past.

She is victimized by her own logic. The future is clear to her and undisturbing, since she trusts the mechanism of cause and effect (Bergson's finalism): if we wish the crown, then what we must do is to murder Duncan; having done so, we attain the end in view. She illustrates the fallacy that so concerned Bergson, believing as she does that she can engineer the future while "the movements constituting the action itself either elude our consciousness or reach it only confusedly." The meaning of her conduct slips away between her clarifications. Each event in her plot sequence has, as Whitehead would say, only a serial relation to other events.

Having heard that Duncan is coming, she voices her confidence in the future:

> Thy letters have transported me beyond
> This ignorant present, and I feel now
> The future in the instant. (I, 5)

This anachronism or ellipsis is not the groping insecurity of Macbeth, who intuits that it is impossible to isolate past from present or future. For Lady Macbeth, whose logic obliterates her sense of guilt, time is not durative but an intelligible and exploitable succession of chronometric incidents. Guilt can be effaced by serial time: "A little water clears us of this deed./How easy is it then." For her there is no fear that a bloody hand will incarnadine the sea. The future is not real for her, but only a mechanical sequence to the present. This mechanistic conception excludes the human meaning of time and ends in an absurdity noted by Whitehead when he asks, "What is the sense of talking about a mechanical explanation when you do not know what you mean by mechanics?"

Lady Macbeth with her logic can repress her guilt as Macbeth cannot. When she walks in her sleep, she reveals that she too experiences a time in which "what's done cannot be undone." But durative time overtakes Lady Macbeth only in her dreams. And she dreams only at night. For her husband the day becomes a waking nightmare when he sees Banquo shaking his gory locks. Lady Macbeth washes her hands only darkling. For her, night does not impinge on day. For Macbeth, the sunlit heavens are stained. For Lady Macbeth,

> the sleeping and the dead
> Are but as pictures.

For Macbeth a man no longer dies when his brains are out but rises again in daylight to "push us from our stools."

We hardly needed Freud to tell us that the dream is timeless. Macbeth's waking nightmare is an existence that exhibits all the anachronism of the primary dream with its condensation of images and time, its psychic displacement, its transforming thought into visual spectra. Having done the deed, Macbeth exclaims that he has murdered sleep. But he did not murder sleep, he merged the night with the day until his life becomes a phantasmagoria of the guilt and trauma that ordinarily release themselves in dreamwork. Sleep is a refuge from chronometric time, but Macbeth's hours are absorbed into the terrible dream that is not a refuge but an inferno. His waking dream proves that he is a moral being who ought to be eligible for tragic experience.

His wife is not a moral being but a clinical case. It is tempting to psychoanalyze Lady Macbeth. When she returns to gild the faces of the sleeping grooms, she explains how she herself would have done the deed had not Duncan resembled her father. This father fixation might account

for her frigidity, making her willing to brain her child
rather than fail in her ambition. Her criminal insensitivity
—what Charcot termed "the beautiful callousness of the
insane"—is perfectly expressed in her invocation to immortal spirits, which are not the chthonic voices Macbeth
heard. She would unsex herself by direst cruelty; she would
thicken her blood until no compunctions of nature could
shake her fell intent; she would have her milk become gall.
These immortal spirits cause her no disturbance such as
afflicts her husband, whose horrible imaginings smother
his thought in surmise and wrench his being apart. Lady
Macbeth's self-control is rational: "These deeds," she
warns, "must not be thought/ After these ways" or we
shall go mad. "Consider it not so deeply," she urges. For
her, reason is an act of repression.

The different parts of her being do not penetrate each
other, as do Macbeth's; the poetry of the dream does not
touch her waking life. She is neurotic; Macbeth is satanic.
Implicit in the play is a distinction between the clinical and
the tragic. Lady Macbeth belongs in the register of characters used by Eugene O'Neill, whose drama submerges
moral dilemmas in clinical analysis. The premises from
which O'Neill works are psychological in the scientific
sense of the term. By contrast, Beckett's strangely distorted
characters are not clinical, but representative of the psychic paralysis or helplessness at the heart of the modern
situation.

By the same token Dostoevsky's fiction constantly moves
back and forth across the border between the clinical and
the ethical. Whatever clinical symptoms may appear in
Raskolnikov, the Raskolnikov experience is radically
moral, not clinical. And of course we sterilize the tragic
action in Sophocles if we insist upon searching for a
mother fixation in Oedipus. It is one of the ironies of our
science that Freud should have affixed to the Sophoclean
tragedy the clinical terminology that belies the meaning of

the play, and doubly ironic that the Oedipal complex should be taken to signify the dramatic meaning of *Hamlet*. Lady Macbeth's dreams are a clinical manifestation, but exactly because of that she is outside the tragic spectrum of her husband's moral struggle. We do not know how Lady Macbeth died; the only hint is that her mind is diseased. Macbeth's mind is not diseased. He is the victim of evil imperatives in his double nature, his diabolic self.

We may see, also, an irony in the fact that time relentlessly closes in on Lady Macbeth, who at night discovers that the past is alive, that the stain will not out, that the old man had more blood in him than she thought, that there's still knocking at the gate. There is a certain interchange of time schemes worked out through the play, Lady Macbeth finally meeting the truth that Macbeth knew from the first —the past impinges on present and future. Meanwhile Macbeth is forced by his successive crimes into a numbness that Lady Macbeth exhibited before the murder, the frigid criminal state in which he forgets "the taste of fears," the fears that once shook his manhood. Yet even when he faces Macduff, Macbeth is still capable of being disturbed, confessing that his

> soul is too much charged
> With blood of thine already.

Macbeth has done "a deed without a name," an act that cannot trammel up the consequences, and one of the recurring Shakespearian themes is the Bergsonian principle that the intellect is unable to cope with our psychic and moral complexities. We cannot think our way through human experience. Shakespeare is continually revising the Cartesian *Cogito, ergo sum* to its opposite: *Sum, ergo cogito.* This was a theme in *Love's Labour's Lost* with its rejection of the academic mastery of life; *Hamlet* plays variations on the same theme. When we let ourselves live, as Bergson says, we live by intensities that are qualitative, not quantitative, and thus not compatible with serial or logical time. The lived life has an anachronistic pace, a fatality in which "what's past is prologue"—but not as the reason comprehends. Lady Macbeth knows how Duncan can be provided for by the great business put in her dispatch:

> Which shall to all our nights and days to come
> Give solely sovereign sway and masterdom. (I, 5)

She is clearer than Iago, who is sadly confused. But she is no more successful.

VI
Patience: Othello

For the ethnologist one of the important indices of a culture is its own kind of awareness of time. Iago contemptuously refers to Othello as a thick-lips, an erring barbarian, and the Moor's own reference to himself indicates that he is black. It seems egregious to read *Othello* ethnologically, and yet this play of total irony is a perhaps unique instance of cultural implications in its opposition of two dissonant time schemes. This circumstance is fundamental to interpreting Shakespeare's most tragic action, for if tragedy means anything, it is to be found in this play. Contrasted with Othello, Oedipus is a formal, almost artificial figure, a remote and "mythical" image of man. Othello is so authentic a human being that any mythical meanings are secondary to his thoroughly realized selfhood, his inalienable grandiose personality which exists in a time scheme different from the time scheme of the Venetian Iago.

One basic difference between so-called primitive cultures and so-called Christian culture is the incompatibility between archaic or cyclic time and the linear or future-oriented time that is apocalyptic or eschatological, the time scheme that is progressive and directed toward a final end. Within the ancient world itself arose an opposition between the cyclical time of the early Greeks—a partly Oriental time that reaches a Great Year, then begins again—

and the historical time born, possibly, of the Hebrew experience of wandering, moving toward a terminus, whether it be a return to the Promised Land, the coming of a Messiah, or, in its later Christian variant, the Second Coming and a Last Judgment.

Perhaps under Greek influence Hebrew thought itself was accommodated to the idea of cyclic time, as *Ecclesiastes* proves: "What has happened will happen again, and what has been done will be done again, and there is nothing new under the sun." The belief that in our beginning is our end had appeared in Heraclitus, who said that the way up and the way down are the same: "In the circumference of the circle the beginning and the end are common."

It has often been pointed out that archaic or cyclic time is ritual time, for the rite is a sacramental act that is not only repeated but is also able to purge man periodically from guilt. The rite duly performed is a symbolic escape from progressive time, and there is nothing novel in the act itself, which must be done again and again in the same way. The sacramental view of time is hardly compatible with the progressive or apocalyptic view of time. Ritual is a form of resistance to linear time, or at least a refuge from it. One of the contradictions within Christian thought is between the necessity of repeating the sacramental rite, which is a recurrent resurrection into another order of being, and the historical or eschatological movement of history to its final end. This contradiction was likewise inherent in Hebrew culture, which was obsessively ritual but, after the exile, was a yearning for a reestablished kingdom.

Vico to the contrary, the fissure between cyclical and progressive time schemes widened after the Renaissance, when under the pressure of ambition, acquisition, and personal initiative, linear or progressive time became symptomatic of the inner-directed self with its neuroses and anxieties, the compulsions of the new economic man. Associated with this drive toward future goals is the discipline or renunciation marking the puritan character with its "worldly asceticism."[1] Sociologists have linked our restlessness with the "Puritan pragmatic syndrome," making time the "great censor of life." Witness our axiom that time is money, our urgent waiting for success. Waiting has become an almost pathological expectation; we wait not only for Godot but in a restlessness that shows our malaise in time, a restlessness that is a kind of irritability. We are afflicted with a quest for novelty while we wait, for the distractions to distract us from our distractions. The eagerness to get to the future means that the old rituals are no longer effective.

Iago has been thwarted by this breakdown in the time-honored ritual of promotion; he has been bypassed in disregard of "old gradation." Yet the old gradation would not have contented him, since he has nothing but scorn for the knee-crooking knave who "wears out his time," doting on his bondage until he is advanced. Such fellows are likely to be cashiered anyhow, he finds, under the new system that promotes Cassio. We speak of the motiveless malignity of Iago. But there is a motive after all, for Iago represents the modern ambitious self that has been frustrated in his ambition. Like characters in Beckett, he is in a situation where he must wait, but he will not wait. He must do something, and is thus driven by his chafing to ingenuities that express his resentment.

In his compulsive time scheme he is a child of his era, and his viciousness should not conceal that he is victim of the urgent Renaissance time scheme that undermined the medieval hierarchical world order. Iago is a far more significant and dangerous figure than Shylock, whose motive took the naive form of greed, a drive to accumulate. Shylock has the Puritan repressions and compulsions associated with thrift, but he is an alien figure, outside the gentile system, and is thus easily expelled. Iago operates within the system itself, the ulcer type who belongs in the very social order that induces his malignity. Iago is not passionless, but his passions are all negative, perverted to rejection.

Iago is motiveless only in the sense that he is quite muddled about his real aims, actually being driven by a desire to disturb any situation that brings peace, stability, or pleasure. He is paranoid in his gnawing suspicions that everybody has victimized him. Cassio has perhaps cuckolded him, Othello has perhaps leapt into his seat, the whole system has bilked him, and he cannot trust anyone. So he must meddle, being irritable and thus ready to exploit the occasion as it offers. Shylock exploits only commercially; Iago exploits the passions of others. He is a figure born of what is now called bad faith in an age of suspicion. Iago suspects himself as well as others, for his sense of not getting his deserts springs from some intuition of his own inferiority. Rejecting himself, he rejects others, a Puritan frame of mind. He is able to transfer this sense of his own inferiority to Othello, who becomes conscious of being black, the blackness that makes him different, and that he must belittle. As image of total rejection or hate, Iago is agent for disorder.

So much is agreed. But from an anthropological view, Iago represents something not individual but cultural, associated with the consuming ambition that came into society with Renaissance initiative: he is the dark face of Leonardo's restlessness, mobility of attention, and incapacity to focus his course in any direction. Leonardo was able to sublimate his restlessness in his art, which was continually experimental and continually inconclusive. Working in many different directions, Leonardo was never interested in reaching any general theory. The unsystematic and opportunistic cast of Leonardo's mind and talent is typical of the diffusion of purpose in Hamlet's petty plotting that unhappily links the Prince with Iago. Leonardo, Hamlet, and Iago all show the disoriented vitality that swings like an unpolarized compass toward momentary aims. Their very individuality is a sign of their temperamental instability, in spite of the fact that they are all driven creatures. They have a directional psychology without having any governing direction.

This unpolarized restlessness stimulated every kind of experimentation, a curiosity to see what happens *if.* According to orthodox Renaissance psychology (a heritage of medieval psychology), the will of such persons has assumed dominance over their reason, and their lively but undirected energy becomes a form of blindness, a loss of final aim, a myopia related to a time scheme in which the immediate future is more clearly conceived than the end. Dante had dealt with this undirected curiosity when he placed Ulysses in the eighth circle of Hell, for Ulysses with his ardor *pour voir* ventured beyond "the end that man should not put out beyond." And Satan seduces Milton's Eve by rousing this kind of curiosity about "experience, best guide." Iago's activist commitment to the next moment is a more malicious pragmatism, and even blinder:

> . . . 'Tis here, but yet confused;
> Knavery's plain face is never seen till used. (II, 1)

The tactic of exploiting the immediate situation in view of a vaguely defined ultimate advantage tinged the new science for which Bacon was spokesman. With innocent optimism Bacon hoped that the method of experiment would make nature the handmaiden of man and bring in Bensalem. Of course Iago has no vision of Bensalem; his experimenting is a perversion of scientific curiosity and ingenuity without any larger purpose than his own advancement, or gaining a sense of his own control over others.

J. T. Fraser comments on the time sense that fixes on the immediate rather than the ultimate. Iago's urgent "now, now, very now" results, at last, in an economy where "it is the process of production itself which becomes the center of interest rather than the product."[2] Industrialism has become "a continuous transition, a permanent revolution" based on a time sense inducing anxiety. Iago is an agent for this permanent revolution within the system. He is a more disturbing and dangerous radical than the subversive activist who would openly upset the *status quo*. He subverts without having any clear vision of an alternative system, and without any moral sanction for his subversion. R. H. Knapp has linked this permanent revolution to the rise of entrepreneurship with its "achievement motivation," which in turn is a symptom of "the Puritan pragmatic syndrome."[3] The urge to exploit the immediate situation without any serious concern for the future is apparent in the reckless unplanned planning of technologists who are committed to the immediate at the expense of the ultimate.

Iago is a puritan in the sense that he cannot tolerate pleasure. He is, in fact, a puritan who can poison all delight. His puritan asceticism is most dangerous whenever he speaks like a moralist, but with satanic intent. He warns Roderigo that if we did not have reason to bridle our sensuality, "to cool our raging motions, our carnal stings, our unbitted lusts," we would be bestial. This sounds like Milton, but Iago's purpose is diabolic. In the same vein Iago (speaking like the purest of moralists) advises Othello that foul thoughts intrude into the cleanest soul. There is a sharp irony in Iago's most pious speeches, for he is always speaking truth without being aware of the truth of what he is speaking, though he knows that he is manipulating a truth. This is Iago's most headlong ignorance.

In classical tragedy the ironic statements are in the mouth of the protagonist (like Oedipus), who speaks ignorantly, not perceiving what he says. The eiron—the Tiresias figure—knows the truth of what the protagonist says, and so does the audience. In *Othello* the irony is compounded, for the eiron, who here is Iago, speaks truth without knowing any better than Othello the validity of what he is saying. In classic tragedy, the good is blind; in *Othello*, evil is also blind. Thus Iago corrupts the Socratic role of questioner or eiron, for Socrates questioned to reach the truth. What Iago intends to sound moral has an evil intent, yet Iago speaks truthfully without recognizing, or caring, that he does so. We see the full meaning, the valid meaning, of what Iago does not see, namely, that foul thoughts can indeed intrude into the purest soul, a principle of puritanism that demands complete honesty and self-scrutiny. Iago is as stupid as Othello, exploiting truth ignorantly and recklessly; he is most honest precisely when he least intends honesty, most credible precisely when he intends to provoke doubt. This is the ultimate perversion of puritanism and the most destructive, an aspect of the opportunism that makes Iago a confused experimenter, confused not only because he is paranoid, but also because he recks not where his experiment is heading.

Had Iago any concern beyond the moment, he would recognize that his meddling is a mortal peril to him, since Othello warns him:

> Villain, be sure thou prove my love a whore!
> Be sure of it; give me ocular proof;
> Or by the worth of mine eternal soul,
> Thou hadst been better have been born a dog
> Than answer my waked wrath! (III, 3)

Or, in dramatic language, Iago is aware that he is playing a role but does not understand the implication of the role he plays. Othello has no awareness of the role in which he is being cast, moving blindly to disaster in this alien role. By contrast, Iago, confessing that he is playing the villain, sees that when the devil puts on his blackest sins, he suggests at first

> with heavenly shows
> As I do now.

But he, too, is moving to disaster.

There is something of the neutrality of the scientific observer in Iago, who disengages himself from the activity he arranges, as if in a laboratory. He plays a role without projecting himself into the drama, for he stands apart as prompter of Othello's cue for passion, casting the roles others are to play without involving himself. To this extent he is a *voyeur*, as the neutral observer was once said to be in science. His manipulation of evidence—proof—is a perversion of the scientific experiment. His questions are put not in the interests of finding truth but, instead, to raise doubts leading to confusion and cynicism.

He leads Othello to destruction by intruding the idea that he must have proof. Having the evidence, Othello can be sure that Desdemona is a whore. So Iago tutors Othello to think objectively. Actually Iago has demonstrated that when they are taken out of context facts are not only deceptive but false. Desdemona did lose the handkerchief, but that does not prove her a whore. When proof—evidence—is removed from a context of belief or good faith, it can only be unreliable or damaging. Here is the situation Hamlet had already discovered, and his last submission ("Let be.") is an attitude based upon what cannot be known: Hamlet has his "proof," but he needs more than proof; he needs trust, faith, belief.

Iago shows the fallacy of naive induction. Whitehead pointed out that induction itself is fruitless; we cannot understand nature by a mere observation of facts, since "there is nothing in the present fact which inherently refers either to the past or to the future." The facts must be treated in a larger context, and to know the facts is not to know the meaning of the facts. The "value" can be found only within a context of conviction, intuition, belief. The need for some context to the "facts" applies in science as well as in the moral life.

John Keats would call this context negative capability:

"that is, when man is capable of being in uncertainties, mysteries, doubts, without any irritable reaching after fact and reason." Iago the irritable provokes this irritability in Othello. Joseph Conrad was always looking for the sort of negative capability he termed steadfastness. In "The Heart of Darkness" he endows the black man with steadfastness; the "savages" keep feeding wood into the furnaces while the boat presses upstream amid a shower of arrows. The monumental figure of the black woman standing silently and enduringly on the shore below Kurtz's palisade is symbolic of the primitive capacity for endurance without irritable reaching after fact and reason. In his native innocence Othello originally had this negative capability, a faculty for trust, belief, acceptance, and everyone else beside Iago is prone to trust. Brabantio trusted Desdemona and regretfully entrusts her to Othello. Cassio trusts; Desdemona trusts Othello's mind.

The deeply disturbing anthropological meaning of the drama is that Iago teaches a great and trusting barbarian to demand proof, to think like a modern positivist. As is always said, when Othello begins to think, he is confused. He thinks his wife is honest, he thinks she is not. So he cries for proof:

> I'll see before I doubt; when I doubt, prove;
> And on the proof there is no more but this—
> Away at once with love or jealousy. (III, 3)

The difference between primitive and modern mentality is that primitive societies do not have to cope with doubt, for their culture is deeply rooted in a fiduciary attitude fringing off into a mentality of acceptance. Trusting would be another term for this attitude. In an essay on modern politics Paul Valéry defined the problem of advanced cultures as reestablishing some "fiduciary structure which is necessary to the whole edifice of civilization," for a valid social structure must have laws deriving their sanction, "their power to compel or restrain," only from this human need for credence, which must underpin codes and reason. Iago demolishes this fiduciary basis of culture.

He teaches Othello to think in exactitudes, to seek evidential facts that undermine his native faculty for trust, for good faith, for love. The penetrating irony is that Iago serves as a commentary on Renaissance pragmatism, which conceals the will to control and which identifies certainty with an "irritable reaching after fact and reason." Iago's tactic of adducing evidence as sufficient unto itself is a facet of a Renaissance culture that became secularized, seeking to know the world as it "is."

Iago is able to name everything exactly—objectively. Love is a lust of the blood, and "the blood is made dull with the act of sport." Physiologically it is. The wine Desdemona drinks is made of grapes. It is. Othello is an erring barbarian. Alas, he is. Iago's honesty is a form of consummate accuracy in naming, denoting, defining, verbalizing. He suffers from the fallacy of specification. His capacity to name is itself a word magic. But naming is not knowing. For Iago, to name is to devalue, to smear. To name is to profane, and Iago has the most profane mind in Shakespeare. He dispels the poetry in Othello's mind and language, and in so doing devastates utterly what Keats called the faery power of unreflecting love.

In *Othello* magic is potent, not only the magic in the handkerchief steeped in mummy, but Iago's designations. By the fallacy of specification Iago perverts language from its sacramental or symbolic uses to the terminology that is nearly behavioristic: Othello and Desdemona are "making the beast with two backs"—now. Othello rejects his barbaric innocence when he urges Iago "give thy worst of thoughts/The worst of words." That is, speak accurately.

Though Iago lies about the evidence, he causes Othello to believe that he sees the world as it "is," which brings crisis. In his book *Mythical Thought,* Ernst Cassirer argues that the primitive mind sees the world magically because it erects no firm barrier between consciousness and the external order. It has no conceptual framework of a world "outside" the self, "objectively." This magical phase of experience, when objects seem "sacred," is modified when the mind recognizes that the outside world is an order not identical with consciousness. Then there comes awareness of a dual reality, the objective and the subjective. So man tries to describe the objective world accurately, to fit it into a rational or coherent scheme by thinking impersonally. The world of ideas is born, and man achieves a conquest by thought.

As Cassirer says, a consciousness of selfdom comes after there is recognition of the limits of the self when faced by the "other" world outside. This consciousness of selfhood is thus the result of a "tragic isolation" from external reality, when man crosses the margin between the innocence of primal experience to a sense of his doubtful situation in another order of being to which he must adjust and from which he is alien. Iago leads Othello across this margin by teaching him to think; and when Othello tries to think, he finds that he is alien—black, different, abused. Othello exclaims, "Farewell the tranquil mind! farewell content!" His occupation is gone. The pun is manifold, not only sexual and military but also anthropological, for his position in the world is no longer secure. He is cast back upon the exactitudes and evidence furnished by Iago, the man who is even more tormented than Othello by the insecurity of his status.

Iago teaches Othello to regard his world from a fixed and limited perspective which is "realistic." Desdemona's handkerchief is found in Cassio's chamber, and she pleads for Cassio, and after all she betrays Brabantio. These are "facts." This realistic point of view has something in it corresponding to the new perspective in Renaissance painting, which organized the "outside" world mathematically as it might be seen from a fixed point of view by a neutral observer. The "visual pyramid" that created a world by geometry placed the beholder outside, and was a quite specious representation of reality, "accurate" though it appeared. Orthogonal perspective destroyed the magic of the earlier ikon, which was a symbolic object of faith rather than a positing of observed actuality. Paul LaPorte has remarked of this artificial perspective, "As art first, then science, began to demythologize nature it became apparent that in the process of this alienation from nature the sense of an encompassing comprehensive world was lost." Renaissance painting was thus evidence of a tragic isolation of the self.

By his conjuration Iago negates the poetry inherent in Othello's primitive world view. The course of this destruction can be traced in the language of the play. At the start Iago and Othello speak different tongues, Iago the realist saying, "Even now, now, very now, an old black ram/ Is tupping your white ewe," Othello speaking his "music." Othello learns to speak Iago's anti-poetic language while at moments Iago, by an almost Bergman-like transfer of *personae*, is able incongruously to speak Othello's poetry:

> Not poppy nor mandragora,
> Nor all the drowsy syrups of the world,
> Shall ever medicine thee to that sweet sleep
> Which thou owedest yesterday. (III, 3)

Meanwhile Othello perverts his own language to Iago's beastly vocabulary: Desdemona is as honest as summer flies in the shambles, and life is a cistern for toads to knot and gender in.

After Othello has learned to call his wife a strumpet, he believes that he has found a reason for murder. It has the name of the Cause (though it cannot be named). The fallacy of exactitude has been extended from the factual evidence to the moral principle driving the Moor to kill in the name of Honor. Iago corrupts not only what Freud called the ego; worse, he endows Othello with a superego, then depraves it. When Othello came to Venice from his barbaric past, he did not have, in his naiveté, a superego. He had lived by the ritual of war in violence which was innocent because it was unconscious. After Iago's tutoring, Othello goes to perform his violent act conscious that he is acting to defend a Cause, countering by action the doubts with which he cannot cope. Freud pointed out that a sense of guilt is the index of civilization, and Iago is able to stimulate in the Moor this cultural or moral sensitivity impelling him to kill in the name of an ethical abstraction.

Driven by his new moral Ideal, Othello acts in behalf of a name, not a thing, for the murder is a deed of mistrust and bad faith. This is only to say that he has been completely muddled by thinking. He has been brought into the situation of civilized men who wage war for a Cause. (John Stuart Mill commented that to go to war for an idea is as criminal as to go to war for territory.[4])

The irony goes further, since the Cause, were it accurately named, is not Honor but a desire newly born in Othello to possess his wife completely—a Iago-like acquisitiveness:

> . . . O curse of marriage,
> That we can call these delicate creatures ours,
> And not their appetites. (III, 3)

Othello has become what Henry James called a beast in a jungle, the predecessor of John Marcher, that cultured gentleman whose unacknowledged drive is to own May Bartram so totally that she is his even after she dies. In acculturating Othello, Iago has turned him into the most treacherous of savages.

The anthropological irony of the play is that the innocent and barbaric Othello should be destroyed by the Venetian code of Iago, a situation that recurs in Conrad's *Heart of Darkness* when Kurtz, the "civilized" western moral agent, reverts to a savagery that is nothing less than total exploitation, driving him from a desire to possess and control to his final ambition to be god. The ultimate phase of Iago's horror is Kurtz, the horror of a perversion that

would make the black man moral while he is being en-
slaved. Kurtz is more dangerous than the savages, whose
lives have an integrity Kurtz has betrayed. Kurtz symbol-
izes too a final phase of the Iago perversion of reason and
morality, and the Iago restlessness.

Iago's amoralism is expressed in his opportunist time
scheme. Iago will not wear out his time, and does not allow
Othello to do so. Desdemona must be strangled tonight,
now, while occasion offers. One of the most disturbing
ironies is the interchange between Othello's primitive time
scheme and Iago's punctual time scheme.[5] Iago's diabolism,
rooted in his confusions, operates by forcing Othello to live
under the tension between two different time schemes, the
urgency of the present moment and the slow, extended
pace of Othello's native time scheme, which is the source
of his magnanimity and endurance. Iago drives the Moor
to think and act in the importunate mode of opportunist,
compulsive time, making a perpetual crisis. When Iago
prompts Othello to conceal himself to watch Cassio, he
promises in his excited and excitable way to make Cassio:

> . . . tell the tale anew—
> Where, how, how oft, how long ago, and when
> He hath, and is again to cope your wife. (IV, 1)

This quickened tempo unsettles the poise of the slow, long-
suffering barbaric mind which almost passively tolerates
what time brings. It disorients the leveling time sense with
which Othello comes to Venice.

There are no novelties in Othello's past, which is a continuum proceeding "from year to year." It is a savage past,
but repetitive, unchanging in its monotony. Othello can
recount what has happened to him only as a succession of
"battles, sieges, fortunes" since he was seven, one so like
another that his experience was monolithic. For Othello
there is little to tell because it is all so cyclic: again and
again, for "such was the process," he says, punning on the

uniformity of his past and the tactic by which he was induced to relate it. The total effect of his narrative is to create a sense of his sufferance—his patience in undergoing such "disastrous chances."

Othello's native patience is a cardinal value in the whole play. His magnanimity, his trust, his capacity for belief, his blind self-assurance are only aspects of the patience with which he takes events as they come. He is disposed to accept what happens without attempting to control it. When Iago prompts him to flee lest he be caught by Brabantio's roused friends, he replies, almost contemptuously, "Let him do his spite," and when Iago draws on Roderigo, Othello disdainfully orders, "Keep up your bright swords, for the dew will rust them." Had it been his cue to fight, he would have known without being prodded. And it is clear from Othello's following account of how he "did thrive in this fair lady's love" that Desdemona "was half the wooer". When she wishes (with double meaning) that heaven had made her such a man, she is exploiting Othello's innocence, as Iago does later. Ironically enough, Desdemona, that seemingly passive girl, speaks of her own "downright violence and storm of fortunes." Though she is, as her father says, still and quiet of spirit, she behaves according to Iago's activist time sense, seizing the moment to win the wild Othello.

The course of events thereafter is set by Othello's conversion to Iago's time scheme, which brings crisis and makes time a symptom of anxiety. There enters Othello's life a new impatience causing him to reject the natural time he previously lived in, the time of endurance: "No! To be once in doubt/Is once to be resolved." In accepting this urgent time scheme Othello loses poise and peace, bringing chaos to a life formerly embroiled but innocent and patient.

One of his most revealing speeches centers on an adverb, for in the first phases of doubt, he turns to Desdemona to remark:

> Excellent wretch! Perdition catch my soul
> But I do love thee! And when I love thee not,
> Chaos is come *again*. (III, 3)

Again: the chaos of his past has been guiltless, but there is
another chaos to come when he learns to act without patience or trust.

Throughout, there is a special anachronism—Othello's
instinct to wait, to endure, not to act upon the moment.
This impulse toward retard is inherent in his savage nature, so that at the very last instant, when he enters Desdemona's chamber to strangle her, there is the pull of his
slow, titanic sense against the moral imperative of his false
and induced civilized superego. There is a monumental
repetition in the rhetoric of "It is the cause, it is the cause."
He will put out the light, then put out the light, and the
conflict in his mind is perfectly phrased in his dim awareness that if he once puts out the light, it will not relume.
The climax of this conflict between his new Iago-like time
and his barbaric patient time is the repetitive "One more,
one more." This retard is not the work of the pauser reason
but of the slow pulse of his nature. It is the almost gravita-
tional drag of his earlier uncorrupted being. But he tells
himself that his sorrow is heavenly, striking where it loves,
so he strangles her—yet slowly. The retard represents the
time of peace which Iago has ruined. It is the retard of a
barbaric mind to which the present is not a crisis, to which
the past is an untroubled process. It is the life rhythm of
one who has not resisted or tried to control time.

The desecration of patience is Iago's most effectual instrument. Under the irritable prompting to act "this night"
and without expostulation, Othello has belied his own
moral nature. Losing his primitive patience, he loses all.
There is something indicative in his speech to Iago explain-
ing that were heaven to try him with the affliction of Job's
sores or give him to captivity without hope, he would have

found in some place of his soul "a drop of patience." But he cannot endure, now, to be a fixed figure for scorn "to point his slow unmoving finger at." With a new hate and mistrust he has learned from Iago, he transforms Patience into a figure of fury:

> . . . turn thy complexion there,
> Patience, thou young and rose-lipped cherubin!
> Ay, there look grim as hell! (IV, 2)

The irony is compounded when Iago, who has taught impatience, urgency, restlessness, keeps preaching patience to both Roderigo and Othello. Again Iago is speaking truth without in the least perceiving, or caring, what the truth is. He entreats Othello to scan matters no further: "leave it to time." And when Othello exclaims that he blows all his love to heaven, committing himself to blood, blood, Iago cautions, "Patience, I say. Your mind perhaps may change." Never does Iago speak more truthfully than when he (diabolically) exhorts Othello:

> How poor are they that have not patience!
> What wound did ever heal but by degrees?
> Thou knowest we work by wit, and not by witchcraft;
> And wit depends on dilatory time. (II, 3)

The use of reason as a moral faculty requires delay. Iago's axiom that wit depends on dilatory time recalls Macbeth's protest that he killed Duncan's grooms in an act that did "outrun the pauser reason." The pauser reason: the moral sanction of reason is not so much to reach truth as to make us pause, to examine, to judge, to hesitate, to make us doubt. The civilized mind, with its heightened self-awareness, faces doubts which apparently do not enter the primitive mind, and reason is the faculty to cope with such doubt. As Hector said in his debate with his Trojan fellows, modest doubt is the beacon of the wise, the hesitation that brings scrutiny.

Primitive as he is, Othello is incapable of using reason,

this civilized "function," which in him is "weak." To think is for Othello disastrous; his "speculative and officed instruments" are inadequate, for he is "perplexed in the extreme." Had he trusted this perplexity, he might have been saved, but under Iago's tutelage he misconceives the proper use of reason, perverting it to a faculty that yields only suspicion and invokes the proof of facts. In short, either his dim reason or the instinct of his blood could have led him to a saving patience. But the perversion of reason corrupts his blood; his thought becomes bloody.

Since he cannot think effectively, Othello has only the function of his blood, and his blood can lead him to either violence or trust. The chaos in his nature was always there, ready to come "again." And it comes "again" when he loses, under Iago's goading, his native capacity for patience, endurance, good faith, belief. It comes when he is befuddled by evidence and cashiers Cassio impulsively. Othello analyzes, unknowing, his own case:

> My blood begins my safer guides to rule,
> And passion, having my best judgment collied,
> Assays to lead the way. (II, 3)

At this moment Othello sees what Iago sees, that he can be an erring barbarian with all the vices of his blood.

So Othello never truly reasons, for his reasoning is a betrayal of reason, and his reliance on "proof" only releases his "other" barbaric self. He has no rational ability to deal with doubt, but only his blood. His blood could have made him spare Desdemona had he yielded to her sweetness, which unprovided his mind. The corruption of Othello's native patience is revealed in his response to Iago's assurance that he can advance proof that Cassio lies with Desdemona:

> . . . Dost thou hear, Iago?
> I will be found most cunning in my patience;
> But—dost thou hear?—most bloody. (IV, 1)

Patience is now put to another use than endurance; it becomes a mode of delay to breed deviousness and plotting. Here we touch the perversion of patience in *Hamlet*, that other play of bad faith, where time gives occasion for windlasses and assays of bias, contrivances, for all the treacheries associated with a quest for proof, and for the mistrust that destroys the fiduciary basis for action. In *Hamlet* patience is only an arena for cunning, knavery, indirections. Until Hamlet says, "Let be," there is a corruption of natural time, the time that eases anxiety, ambition, and disruption—the time of "continuity." Othello is a far simpler figure than Hamlet, who ends where Othello began, for when Othello came to Venice, time was trust, bringing no apprehension, malaise, or compulsion. Then under Iago's urging, his time becomes an agent of disintegration.

Iago, who disorients everybody, succeeds in working an interchange between his time scheme and Desdemona's, just as he works an interchange in Othello. After Cassio is dismissed, Desdemona adopts Iago's impatient, urging time: now, now. She assures Cassio that she will pressure Othello for his immediate reinstatement:

> I'll watch him tame and talk him out of patience;
> His bed shall seem a school, his board a shrift;
> I'll intermingle everything he does
> With Cassio's suit. (III, 3)

This is unwise, and has the punctual tempo of Iago's where, how, how oft, how long ago. Desdemona reasons with Othello as Iago does, insisting by repeated questions: Shall it be shortly? Tonight? Tomorrow, dinner?

> Why then, tomorrow night, or Tuesday morn,
> On Tuesday noon or night, or Wednesday morn.
> I prithee name the time. (III, 3)

Again word magic: the will to control time by designating the instant when.

Ironically Desdemona is meanwhile advising Cassio patience, for her advocacy is not in tune—"You must a while be patient," which simply echoes Iago's cunning advice to Othello: "Confine yourself but in a patient list." And while Desdemona is teaching Cassio patience, Iago is recommending patience to Roderigo, who has been daffed with devices. Yet Iago promises Roderigo that he will enjoy Desdemona the next night after Cassio is murdered.

When this play is compared with *Hamlet* an overarching irony is that the time lag is damaging in Denmark whereas it is what would have saved everything in Cyprus. Hamlet needs to act, but action in Cyprus is the release of Othello's blacker disposition, or else the blind improvising of a Iago who does not see where he is going but knows that he is on his way. Othello is led to think he knows where he is going, and by the quickest way; he will strangle her: "Iago, this night. I'll not expostulate with her, lest her body and beauty unprovide my mind again. This night, Iago!" Othello's mind is most unprovided when he thinks, when he has proof, which is as futile in Cyprus as it is in Denmark, and as irrelevant when it is given out of context. What is past reason hunted is past reason hated. Othello is never more deluded than when he believes Iago's assurance:

> . . . let me know;
> And knowing what I am, I know what she shall be. (IV, 1)

Knowledge based upon proof by exact naming is an Iago-irrationalism. By this violation of reason and time Iago destroys all idyllic relations and causes a cynicism that eats into that other drama of disillusion, *Troilus and Cressida*, a play again dealing with doubt and reason and opening a fissure between moral and intellectual experience.

VII

Space, Time, and Duty:
Troilus and Cressida

In recent scientific theory time appears under two opposite aspects: in the behavior of the particle moment by moment, as if it were free, and in the behavior of a multitude of particles in a statistical pattern which covers a span of time and can be formulated in a probability graph that denotes necessity. The Brownian movement illustrates: in a given solution the particles will all within a certain period sink to the bottom, but within this period any given particle will sink at its own erratic rate and by its own path, as if it had a measure of freedom. Time, for it, is an index of a certain autonomy, but time for all the particles is an index of necessity when reckoned by the laws of precipitates. We can predict the total movement even if we cannot predict the movement downward of any one particle. Thus long-range time signifies necessity, whereas the behavior of the particle at any instant signifies a degree of freedom. This double guise of time means a kind of choice for individual particles in the present, but determinism for many particles in the future. Without the behavior of the individual particles necessity is, as Whitehead says, only an abstraction, and the behavior of individual particles is meaningless without the abstract law determining how particles behave in the solution.

In graphing the total movement of the particles, we translate time to spatial representation. When time is thus spatialized, it betokens necessity; when it is not spatialized, it represents contingency. The laws of Newtonian physics were subject to a vivid spatial imagination, but Newton was less successful in dealing with the contingencies of time and tended to spatialize his cosmic order in a diagram of physical laws of push and pull. The laws of our world are not now the absolute, undeviating laws of Newtonian physics but, instead, the laws of probability; and probabilities work themselves out through contingencies, which can be represented statistically even if no statistician expects his graphs to apply to each instance at any moment.

That is, the scientist no longer treats freedom and necessity as if they were polar, mutually exclusive opposites, since any law of atomic activity may not apply to the relatively unpredictable state of the particle at a given moment. For the particle is determined in prospect but conditionally free at present. This freedom does not cancel necessity, and, more important, the eventual necessity gives meaning and value to the freedom of the immediate occasion. The value of freedom derives, precisely, from the inevitabilities lying ahead and endowing the particle at the moment with its own identity. If the structure of the atom can be conceived as a spatial design—a pattern of destined activity statistically defined on a long-range time scale—its actual existence instant by instant is a mode of resisting this large-scale time pattern, which is necessity. In its course of existence in time the atom consequently expresses, or fulfils, both its freedom and its destiny. Its spatial design corresponds to the necessities of its history; its present state corresponds to its independence.

Thus the structure of the hydrogen atom is a statistical contour to which at the moment it may not conform. And since statistical contours can be diagrammed only on an extended timescale, the statistical definition of atomic structure is spatializing the atom's existence in time. Statistical formulations are the modern guise of determinism, which means, in effect, that inevitabilities are spatial, tranforming time to graphs, norms, curves, abstract designs. Yet the personal, private, and existential meaning and value are not these statistical contours—not in space, but in the momentary release of the individual from these contours.

In this sense, then, we are determined in space but free in time. Paul Fraisse has said that while space is imposed upon us, the conquests of personality are made in time. The scientist Satosi Watanabe has echoed, regarding our probabilistic view of things, that "Space is the vehicle of determination . . . , time is the vehicle of freedom and value."[1] And speaking of Elizabethan drama, Tom Driver observes that "Shakespeare's view of time is inseparable from his view of freedom." The existentialist tradition in modern thought treats the crisis of the instant as more significant than any assigned destiny, and since each instant requires an either/or choice, man's fate is a reflex of his momentary choices, just as the structure of the atom emerges from its momentary behavior. The local, the contingent are not adventitious, but are the basis from which the laws of probability generate abstract necessities. The present is the ground of individual experience, making, as Kierkegaard says, the particular superior to the universal. In Karl Jaspers's words, "An indispensable approach to the truth would be lost without the exceptions." So, also, Whitehead repeats that the salvation of reality is its ultimate matter-of-fact concreteness, which asserts itself momentarily.

Apart from *Antony and Cleopatra*, *Troilus and Cressida*, above all other Shakespearean plays, is the one having a special juxtaposition of space and time, the idea of a hierarchical world order—the so-called Elizabethan world picture—being disintegrated by the injurious effects of time upon this world order through the devastations of Mutability. The hierarchical world view requires that each one should have, and keep, his place "in all line of order," a half-medieval system that would, from the modern view, diminish the scope of freedom. According to this half-feudal view, essentially spatial, evil is the act that unsettles this degree. Ulysses's speech on order shows what follows when this spatial hierarchy is disrupted by the unruly wills of men, when power degenerates into appetite, doubly seconded by will, and makes an universal prey that at last eats up itself.

This unchecked power, associated with the new Machiavellian politics, was a prospect that frightened the Renaissance, and its consequences are felt in *Troilus and Cressida*, in the wilful politics of Paris and those who would keep Helen, and in the final hate of the disillusioned Troilus, who turns savage in his quest for revenge. The destruction of a world order is the special theme of *Lear*, but *Troilus and Cressida* is more complex, for it is a study in both space and time—the demolition of a world order by the wrackful siege of battering days. The grim theme is voiced in Agamemnon's words:

> What's past and what's to come is strewed with husks
> And formless ruin of oblivion. (IV, 5)

The play crystallizes differing responses to the rage of Time, with which neither Beauty nor Honor can hold plea. It is a point of intersection between the inherited spatial world view and the new temporal world view, a paradigm of temporal experience newly realized. In his two speeches on order and on time, Ulysses phrases the paradigm; his discourse on the need for order stands over against his cynical speech on the urgency of time, that compulsive time sense associated with individual initiative: "Take the instant way," for emulation is the law of life, a commitment to Mutability. When the old spatial, hierarchical order is undermined by Mutability, the meaning of freedom alters, depending on how one maintains himself against Time and Change. Time can be either freedom or necessity, a theatre in which the moral life is either thwarted or fulfilled. Shakespeare is dealing with a crisis in Renaissance culture.

The old spatial world order is symbolized in Dante's *Commedia* with its premise that sin is whatever takes degree away. This sense of priority and place was inherited from the Ptolemaic view of the world seen *sub specie aeternitatis*. Dante's is the spatial ethic of a feudal age. Newton's later reorganization of this hierarchical order was really only a secular revision of the Dantesque system, as spatially constructed as the spheres of medieval science. The universe was ordered by the laws of physics instead of the will of God. Under Newtonian laws of dynamics time itself was spatialized in the form of absolute time. As Joost Meerloo writes, "The Newtonian idea of time represented perfect and universal ordering. . . . Cosmic time was defined as an entity by itself, irrespective of events," for all local time was measured against this absolute time, which was a manifestation of the constant geometry of the universe.[2] Newton himself stated:

> Absolute, true, and mathematical time, of itself and from its own nature, flows equably without relation to anything external . . . ; relative, apparent, and common time is some sensible and external (whether accurate or unequable) measure of duration by the means of motion, which is commonly used instead of true time, such as an hour, a day, a month, a year.

In Newton, local time was merely adventitious, not real and circumstantial. But Shakespeare knew that time is a mortal rage, defacing life.

In short, Newton did not succeed in bringing into his world order the great time dimension that is the variable in modern experience; he simply subtracted from the cosmos the religious and moral imperatives inherent in the medieval and Elizabethan spatial cosmos. At the onset of the Enlightenment, Addison was still basing his quasi-deistic vision on the spacious firmament, a celestial geometry; and Pope's great chain of being was an order as hierarchical as Ulysses's spatialized insisture, course, and form. In fact, the entire Enlightenment was dominated by a spatial imagination, by a vision of a cosmic system with which man must cooperate.

It was not until the romantic experience that time finally disrupted this spatial order. It was left for Wordsworth to speak of "the unimaginable touch of time"; Schopenhauer knew that "our self-consciousness has not space as its form, but only time"; and Amiel called time "the successive dispersion of being." During the 19th century the sense of individual being became so closely associated with time that Amiel sees himself "only as a fugitive appearance." Time, for him, "is nothing but the inner prism through which we diffract being and life." Existentialism, with its anxiety about the crisis of the instant, is a last phase of a concern with time that entered the Renaissance with the Calvinist belief that we all exist in momentary peril under the judgment of an almighty God.

So the conception of a cosmic spatial order may not be, after all, "the most characteristic" feature of the Renaissance mentality. The most characteristic—or the most radical—feature may be, instead, a new awareness of time, which broke open, if it did not destroy, the established spatial vision. The whole Renaissance can be taken as a field of contest between a spatial and a temporal view of reality.

Long before Newton, painters and architects, in their quest for mathematical proportion, were attempting to impose a spatial order on art. The reliance on the golden measure (1/1.618) in architecture and sculpture was evidence of this concern for an ideal spatial measure, and

Rudolf Wittkower has proven that mathematical harmonies dominated the design of the period, which accepted Pythagorean theories of number as absolutes. In painting, orthogonal perspective was a kindred abstract spatial system.

Always pulling against these spatial systems was a heightened sense of time and its destructions, mutations, illusions, and disillusions. Leonardo exclaims:

> O time, swift despoiler of created things, how many kings, how many peoples hast thou undone, how many changes of states and circumstances have followed since the wondrous form of this fish died here in this cavernous and winding recess.
>
> O time, consumer of all things! O envious age, thou destroyest all things and devourest all things with the hard teeth of the years little by little, in slow death. Helen, when she looked in her mirror and saw the withered wrinkles which old age had made in her face wept and wondered why she had twice been carried away.[3]

With this sense of time came a feeling for the individual and contingent, for the *uomo singolare*, the illusory blue distance, dreamlike, opening behind the figures in Leonardo's painting, which represented the world in the twilight Leonardo loved. Beyond the geometry of Renaissance painting there were transitory visions of fantastic landscapes. Leonardo's grotesque faces are records of fleeting expressions. The Renaissance interest in the local and momentary was doubtless a continuation of the gothic analysis of light under changing atmospheric conditions—the fleeting radiance falling through the flamboyant mathematic of a cathedral or playing over the gray surface of a facade. Then the Renaissance chiaroscuro and local cast light changed the fabric of reality seen at an instant, dissolving it in a luminous climate. Above all, as Panofsky argued, the Renaissance had a new sense of its temporal distance from

the classical era, producing in the artist and scholar a nos-
talgia for the past, unlike the living presence of the past in
the medieval sculpture or in Dante. The middle ages foreshortened history; personages from the past were represented as medieval. In spite of its Platonic sense of what is
timeless, the Renaissance felt that the past was bygone;
thus its vision of ancient Rome was elegiac—a dream of a
different age and order.

So, as Tillyard notes, the medieval world order survived
in a precarious state, and a great many Elizabethans put up
a rear guard action to defend it against the disintegrating
forces that Hiram Haydn terms the counter-Renaissance.
Elyot's *Book of the Governor* is such a rear guard defense,
anticipating what Ulysses says: "Take away order from all
things, what should then remain? Certes nothing finally,
except some man would imagine eftsoons chaos." Spenser's
"Hymn of Heavenly Beauty" describes the cosmos as a
spatial structure embodying the golden ratio of Renaissance architecture:

> And as these heavens still by degrees arize,
> Untill they come to their first Mover's bound,
> That in his mightie compasse doth comprize,
> And carrie all the rest with him around,
> So those likewise doe by degrees redound,
> And rise more faire, till they at last arrive
> To the most faire, whereto they all do strive.

The sense of temporality ate into this essentially spatial
scheme, as Spenser knew when he turned to the Mutability
cantos, which set the theme of *Troilus and Cressida,* for Mutability is destructive:

> Ne shee the lawes of Nature onely brake,
> But eke of Justice, and of Policie;
> And wrong of right, and bad of good did make, . .
> And all this world is woxen daily worse.
> O pittious worke of MUTABILITIE.

Or, as Ulysses put it, high birth, vigor, and love are victims of calumniating time. In *Troilus and Cressida* the high-minded values of the Renaissance are cancelled.

Although this drama examines in a variety of ways the sundry injuries of Time, Shakespeare at last, in the character of Hector, implies that there is a mode of resistance to the Mutability so damaging to the other personages. Hector's mode of resistance by his commitment to duty strangely anticipates some of our modern conceptions of freedom. Otherwise the play puts up no rear guard action against Change, but is penetrated by a cynicism about human beings immersed in Time that is destructive to every value. The insecurity of all the characters except Hector is due to the profound disturbance entering Renaissance consciousness when modern man is plunged into what Carlyle calls the time element.

Troilus and Cressida is a declamatory play, almost theoretic in its ethical and philosophical debate, which sets it apart as an ideological drama.[4] In fact, the action develops almost into a design of philosophical positions, and we suspect that Shakespeare here wrote for an educated and sophisticated audience. Here the rational life stands over against the moral life, for the play explores the gap between the intellectual and the moral, and the moral action concerns how the characters submit to, exploit, or resist change and time, creating their own values in the flux of mutability and destiny. The ethical meanings attach not so much to the theme of order as to the various ways of coping with the time that defeats, for, as Agamemnon says, "The ample proposition that hope makes . . . Fails in the promised largeness."

In this play time is the authentic field of human experience. One of the finest contrasts in an otherwise callous drama is the opposition of lived time, which is inaccessible to reason, and merely thought time, which is so amenable to reason that it leads certain characters either to absurd idealism or else to an easy and superficial cynicism. Cressida and Hector are the ones helpless before lived time, which casts them back upon themselves in two different sorts of irrationalism, whereas Paris, Troilus, Agamemnon, and Ulysses are able, each in his own way, to conceptualize time and in so doing are led either to romantic idealism or to a kind of pragmatism that is little different from the cynicism of Diomedes.

Cressida is driven to her own brand of cynicism by her consciousness that time wears away everything—security, confidence, love. In effect she reaffirms what has been said by the Player King in *Hamlet*, that what we intend we often abandon, since purpose is a slave to mere memory and of poor validity. Cressida's most characteristic complaint is addressed to Troilus after their night together: "Prithee tarry. You men will never tarry." Her fear of the insecurity of the present underlies her cynicism, causing her to spy more dregs than water in their love even before it is consummated, and in her very fears she finds safer footing than in any "blind reason stumbling without fear." For "to fear the worst oft cures the worse." Cressida, in fact, has almost no defense against the abrasions of time.

She knows herself for what she is, a woman "slyding of corage," as Chaucer had it. In the sordid nocturnal episode when she gives the sleeve to Diomedes, she surrenders the token with the full sense that it was impossible for her to keep it anyhow even if Diomedes takes her fidelity with it. So she yields it with the sad perception that it was given her by one "that loved me better than you will." She resigns herself to her treachery with an entirely self-aware judgment that capitulates to the fatality of the passing moment:

> Well, well, 'tis done, 'tis past. And yet it is not;
> I will not keep my word. (V, 2)

Usually Cressida is taken as only a daughter of the game, a sluttish spoil of opportunity. Yet she is not really a whore, whatever accosting welcome she may give to the next comer. She is a girl whose only value can be the pleasure of the present moment because she is, she knows, alone before time, the injurious thief of reason, purpose, devotion, loyalty. As Robert Ornstein says, "More realist than sensualist, more wary and weary than wanton, she is alone in Troy and defenseless among the Greeks." She can salvage from her experience only the fleeting sensations that are solace for her desolation.

This is what links her with Emma Bovary, that other hedonist whose dreams are often sentimental, and whose will to believe is corrupted by the disillusions of experience. When Emma is finally and crushingly aware that Léon, too, has slipped away, she has Cressida's response, Léon suddenly seeming to her as far away as the others: " 'Yet I love him,' she said to herself. No matter! She was not happy—she never had been. Whence came this insufficiency in life—this instantaneous decay of everything on which she leaned?" It is Cressida's question, and Emma's response is as desperate as Cressida's when she is told that she must, all at once, go to the Greeks. She will dote on the exuberance of her sentimental grief, which Pandarus urges her to moderate:

> Why tell you me of moderation?
> The grief is fine, full, perfect that I taste,
> And violenteth in a sense as strong
> As that which causeth it. How can I moderate it?
> If I could temporize with my affections,
> Or brew it to a weak and colder palate,
> The like allayment could I give my grief. . . . (IV, 4)

One recalls Keats's hedonism in the "Ode on Melancholy," where he bursts joy's grape against his fine palate, turning it to poison, the aching pleasure that is a perversion because the strenuousness of his effort is defeated by his sense that Beauty must die. All that is left to salvage is the luxury of the grief itself, a form of despairing self-indul-

gence in a world where honey turns to gall as it is tasted.
Cressida has her moment of such romantic rebellion
against the poison of time when the news comes that she
must leave Troilus:

> . . . Time, force, and death,
> Do to this body what extremes you can,
> But the strong base and building of my love
> Is as the very center of the earth. . . . (IV, 2)

Yet she knows that this is mere rhetoric: "I'll go in and
weep." She knows she will not be loyal. This vulgar but
very human sense of her weakness saves Cressida from
being a mere slut.

Unlike everyone but Hector, Cressida can be hurt by
time, and in a play so insolent it is commendable to be
susceptible to injury and to recognize one's own fallibility.
Cressida has her own kind of honesty, a reason grounded
in her shallow heart which the rationalism of others cannot
know. Her hedonism or, more accurately, her epicureanism, is testimony, however devalued, to her being in the
human condition, or at least *a* human condition. The horizon of the epicurean is limited to the present, for she does
not have the freedom of a Cleopatra, that glittering queen
who was also a hedonist but whose vision could project her
toward the eternal. Cressida is not free, though she is able,
even in her helpless position, to choose. She makes a wrong
choice, we say, but it is a choice of which she is sadly aware,
a capitulation to fortune.

A degree of pathos attaches to this wanton girl, who sees
more clearly than Emma Bovary where she is and who can
conceive the treachery with which time wears away her
satisfactions of the moment. When she protests to Troilus
that she will not be false, she passes judgment on herself in
a poetry to which her nature is not equal:

> When time is old and hath forgot itself,
> When waterdrops have worn the stones of Troy,

> And blind oblivion swallowed cities up,
> And mighty states characterless are grated
> To dusty nothing, yet let memory
> From false to false, among false maids in love
> Upbraid my falsehood. (III, 2)

This protest does not help her, for her truer wisdom is in her confession that to love is to be a fool. One has an impossible choice—either to love or be wise,

> . . . for to be wise and love
> Exceeds man's might; that dwells with gods above.

So she yields to time, and in contrast to her merely rhetorical idealism she is driven back upon the only reasoning available to her—cynicism: "I will not keep my word." Cynicism and pathos fuse in her experience.

Cressida is concessive to the changes of lived experience as Troilus is not, for he makes his own conquest of time. First he believes utterly in his own abiding loyalty; then, when disillusioned, he commits himself to unchanging hate, a change from idealism to savagery. These false conquests are really escapes from time—positions so inflexible that they blind him to actuality, adaptability, resignation. Both his idealism and savagery are injurious. At the start Troilus is so deluded by his idealism that he holds an image of Cressida as a pearl whose bed is India, a self-deception reminding us of Shelley's view of Emilia Viviani when he wrote "Epipsychidion"—the Emilia who turned out to be not a Juno but a cloud, as he later confessed. Addicted to his idealistic vision of Cressida, Troilus feels himself exempt from the ravages of infidelity; he stands secure in the mirror image of his own devotion: "Fear not my truth." In the face of Cressida's doubt, Troilus proclaims that "what truth can speak truest" is "not truer than Troilus."

In the course of time this idealist becomes a madman, like Theseus's lover and poet, and when he sees Cressida give the sleeve to Diomedes, he affirms that there is a revolt so strong in his heart that it inverts the testimony of eyes and ears. This is not Cressida, she is not there before him, she does not give the sleeve away. Or if she did, the infidelity smirches all women, even his mother. Within his soul is a fight so dire that reason rebels against the evidence; or else the evidence breaks the very bonds of heaven, and his whole world collapses into absurdity. In desperation Troilus swivels from idealism to malice:

> . . . as much as I do Cressid love,
> So much by weight hate I her Diomed. (V, 2)

So he will leave pity with his mother when he fights the Greeks, and he reproaches Hector for showing mercy to the fallen, tempering his wrath. Hector makes the suitable comment on this conversion from one absolutism to another: "Fie, savage, fie."

In either guise, idealist or savage, Troilus the romantic fixates his posture. The two aspects of this romantic absolutism are evident in Shelley, whose vision of man is Promethean, exempt from change and fate. Then his savagery appears in the ode to the west wind, proclaiming that if he had power—the power that would brook no resistance —he could save the world by the tyranny of his fierce spirit. Beneath this fierceness is a cynicism on which power operates; or if not cynicism, despair.

Troilus had moments when he might have become as humanly weak as Cressida. His very idealism, mistaking Cressida for a pearl, veils a sensuality, much as Shelley's pseudo-Platonic vision of woman in "Alastor" and "Epipsychidion" veiled his sensuality. For Troilus confesses to Pandarus that he is giddy with expectation of his night with Cressida; he is enchanted by the imaginary pleasure:

> . . . some joy too fine,
> Too subtle, potent, tuned too sharp in sweetness

> For the capacity of my ruder powers
> I fear it much; and I do fear besides
> That I shall lose distinction in my joys. . . . (III, 2)

At this moment Troilus is tinged with Cressida's vulnerable epicureanism, like Keats cherishing the exquisite sensations that are a commitment to lived time. Some of Cressida's concession to the flesh, or her "slyding corage," might have saved Troilus.

And when Troilus parts so hastily from her, he is momentarily infected by the human dread and mistrust in which she exists—a distrust of herself and the course of events. As he gives her the sleeve, he hesitates:

> But something may be done that we will not;
> And sometimes we are devils to ourselves
> When we will tempt the frailty of our powers,
> Presuming on their changeful potency. (IV, 4)

Yet this alley to doubt closes at once to Troilus's absolutist mind, and he discounts all chance of mutability. When Cressida asks whether he will be faithful, he ironically replies that he catches only simplicity by his great truth. So Troilus protects himself against time by his vision of love, then by his unchanging hatred. Both are inhumane compared with Cressida's sense of the precariousness of passing moods.

In some ways Diomedes resembles Troilus by being invulnerable, for Diomedes is the cynic *sang pur,* who never had any ideals to lose and thus is exempt from the injuries of time and change. When Troilus asks Diomedes to use Cressida well while she is with the Greeks, he replies bluntly, "When I am hence/I'll answer to my lust." Entirely without illusions, Diomedes belongs by his nature to the abusive and disabused Greek world in which he so easily lives. He seizes the occasion as it comes, and like Cressida takes the moment for what it is worth, though unlike Cressida he cannot be hurt. He too lives deeply in passing time, but exploits it for his own interest. If Cressida seizes the pleasure of the moment, she lacks the confidence of a Diomedes, whose exploitations are more effective than hers because he is less sensitive. Diomedes survives to win; Cressida survives to lose. However it sullies, her survival is a precautionary activity. She is saddened by her very defense against time's outrage. Diomedes's cynicism lacks the melancholy that beclouds Cressida's impure satisfactions; he is the debauched, not Cressida.

Cressida is weak in will. By contrast, Paris, like Troilus, makes consciousness an absolute defense against time, subjecting it to the tyranny of thought, which in this instance is an aspect of the will. Paris and Troilus master time by imposing upon it a vision that makes honor and love absolute values. In the great debate during the second act they argue that Helen must be kept for the sake of Trojan honor. Even if it was wrong to take her from Menelaus, the very wrong transforms itself to an honorable act if she can be held: "I would have," says Paris,

> the soil of her fair rape
> Wiped off in honorable keeping her.
> Were I alone to pass the difficulties,
> And had as ample power as I have will,
> Paris should ne'er retract what he hath done. . . . (II, 2)

Troilus supports this wilful policy, agreeing that the Trojans cannot blench "to stand firm by honor."

For them, honor is inflexibility in an admittedly wrong cause. They imply that no error should be rectified if one has the power to maintain it. This could be called stubbornness; or we can say that Troilus and Paris have made their will lord of their reason in a brand of idealism that amounts to a vicious immorality. A great deal of romanticism which passes for idealism is actually irrationality of that kind, as Hamlet knew. It is an irrationalism that denies the reality of time's reversals. For Paris and Troilus, Helen becomes an abiding symbol of Trojan honor:

> A spur to valiant and magnanimous deeds,
> Whose present courage may beat down our foes
> And fame in time to come canonize us. (II, 2)

To keep Helen in honor's name arrests the course of time and perverts history into a record of insane causes that have been successfully defended: *Weltgeschichte ist Weltgericht.* When Hector points out the illegality of the rape, Troilus reproaches him: it is a base theft "that we have stolen what we do fear to keep."

This finding honor in a straw is nothing less than an act of establishing the world as one's idea of the world, an exploitation of time in the name of an ideal. It veils a cynicism not far from the cruder cynicism of Diomedes, who answers his lust as he pleases. Both are variants of power philosophies that subject reason to will or appetite. Paris and Troilus foreshadow a romantic imperialism of the mind that makes the world identical with their idea of the world. Their idealism disguises their wilful pragmatism, the insistence that honor accrues from success.

Pragmatism in another vein appears in Ulysses, whose shrewd mind is concerned only with results. Properly speaking, Ulysses should be called an opportunist rather than a pragmatist, for he keeps his eye always on the main chance, and more than anyone in the play can manipulate his high-sounding principles for present advantage. With his worldly wisdom, which sounds like morality, Ulysses is best able to exploit time by a tactical mastery of the occasion. Although he is given to mouthing precepts, and eloquently too, he is ethically a cynic more objectionable than Diomedes. His impressive advice seems to have a gravity that makes old Nestor merely quaint, yet he is prepared to belie his own moralizing as soon as he can turn the moment to account.

Upon his first appearance, for example, Ulysses delivers himself of the most-quoted passage in Shakespeare upon the necessity of order, degree, and priority: when this de-

gree is shaked, the universe shatters and enterprise is sick.
But before the scene is done, Ulysses urges that Ajax, not
Achilles, be commissioned to fight Hector even though
Achilles is the nobler man. This tactic is, Ulysses argues,
justified by a salesman's trick: show your foulest wares first
and, if they do not sell, then offer the better. So "by device"
blockish Ajax may perchance win and the insolent Achilles
be disciplined.

Behind this policy—a corruption of the very principle of
degree and order—is a misconception blinding Ulysses almost as the idealist Troilus is blinded. Neither Ulysses nor
Troilus sees Cressida for what she actually is, a weak and
commonplace woman with a certain reduced sensitivity. If
Troilus thinks she is a pearl, Ulysses sees only her sensuality. As Cressida comes to the Greeks, Ulysses passes the
obvious judgment that she is a mere baggage:

> Fie, fie upon her!
> There's language in her eye, her cheek, her lip;
> Nay, her foot speaks. Her wanton spirits look out
> At every joint and motive of her body. (IV, 5)

As indeed they do. Yet that is not the whole truth about
Cressida, as we know in her other transactions. Ulysses
makes a knowing but coarse appraisal of this shopworn and
unfortunate girl.

Ulysses's pragmatism is more obvious in his magnificently rhetorical lines on time, which again are spoken
with tactical purpose, directed at the pompous Achilles.
There is something nearly Iago-like in Ulysses' maxim that
unless the moment is seized, time devalues man. Iago
speaks with the same compulsiveness as Ulysses, who urges
"the instant way," otherwise reputation tarnishes. Far
from holding that virtue arises from stable and established
merit, Ulysses cynically proposes that it is a matter of reputation, and reputation is a perishable commodity, quickly
obsolescent. His grandiloquent and memorable speech al-

most says what the disabused Stalinist critics said: history is written for the moment only. For Time has a wallet in which to discard the esteem won in the past; perseverance alone keeps honor bright; virtue itself cannot win abiding respect; and beauty, wit, meritorious service, "love, friendship, charity are subjects all/To envious and calumniating time."

The course of time is little more than slander, and merit is won in an enterprise so transitory that the narrow gate to reputation admits only one at a given moment, and all this in a moil of competition where the hindmost are trampled. Time is as importunate for Ulysses as it is for Iago, although Ulysses is never called to account for his rhetoric, and Iago is. Ulysses is a more privileged exploiter of time than Iago. Unlike Cressida, he cannot be penalized by time, since he is on the winning side.

The strangeness of this play is that it is premised upon an assumption of world order, and yet the conception of an abiding order is corroded by the scandal of time, which plunges the characters into defection, converts Troilus to savagery, catches Hector unarmed, and makes Pandarus delay bequeathing his pox to the audience now. It is a play of betrayed hopes, diseased romance; a cancelling of all promising expectation, strewing oblivion everywhere. Against the ravage of time there seems nothing that could be called freedom unless it be to exploit the moment with Ulysses.

Nevertheless despite all this ruination there is a suppressed and oblique affirmation of human freedom as it is understood today—a freedom that is a mode of resistance to time—in Hector's experience. Hector, like Cressida, has everything to lose in this ruthless drama of inevitable disappointments inflicted by "injurious time" cramming up his rich thievery and drenching all fidelity with "the salt of broken tears." The salt of tears is the only tragic value in this callous and desolating action. They are shed by An-

dromache and Cassandra when they try to persuade Hector
not to arm.

Hector replies to their plea by seeming to speak like
Troilus or Paris; he will sally forth because he is committed
to a principle of honor that "keeps the weather" of his fate:

> Life every man holds dear, but the dear man
> Holds honor far more precious-dear than life. (V, 3)

This honor is not the honor that Troilus and Paris have
invoked, and the reason is clear when Priam too urges how
"this day is ominous," causing Hector to answer:

> I must not break my faith.
> You know me dutiful; therefore, dear sir,
> Let me not shame respect, but give me leave
> To take that course by your consent and voice. (V, 3)

"You know me dutiful"—the meaning of Hector's sense of
duty, his commitment to Troy, appears when Ulysses tells
him how inevitable it is that Ilium will fall to the Greeks,
since these towers that buss the clouds "must kiss their own
feet." Ulysses speaks with the sanction of the gods' ordi-
nance, yet Hector counters with a profession that is not
belief in the usual sense but, instead, an act that William
James might call the will to believe:

> There they stand yet, and modestly I think
> The fall of every Phrygian stone will cost
> A drop of Grecian blood. The end crowns all,
> And that old common arbitrator Time
> Will one day end it. (IV, 5)

The speech is one that might be spoken by Dr. Rieux or
Tarrou in Camus's *The Plague*. For neither of these men has
any genuine hope of checking the epidemic or, perhaps, of
even surviving it. Yet they treat the infected in Oran and
behave as if they were free to choose. Their position in the
diseased city is an act of resistance to a fatality they clearly

recognize; they are entirely aware of the statistical graph over which the course of an epidemic must proceed. Their ministration is an opposition, absurd and modest enough, against time and the curves of pathology. Sisyphus, too, knows that when he has rolled his stone to the height, it will roll down again, and his only response is to rebel against this determinism. Or as Ortega y Gasset puts it, our destiny when we come into the world obliges us to choose: "To live is to feel ourselves *fatally* obliged to exercise our *liberty*, to decide what we are going to be in this world. Not for a single moment is our activity of decision allowed to rest. Even when in desperation we abandon ourselves to whatever may happen, we have decided not to decide."[5]

Sisyphus was scornful in the face of fatality. Hector is not scornful. He is behaving modestly, as he says, according to a moral imperative that is his act of freedom—a choice imprudently made in the face of what he knows is fated.[6] Thus the gap opens between his intellectual and his moral recognitions. The freedom of his existence appears within this gap. He alone of all the characters in the play has the privilege of acting with such freedom, a freedom that arises from obligation as a Trojan and a man.

The night before Agincourt Hal faced the obligation to make a similar commitment, a commitment that for him, also, endorsed his freedom. But Hal made his choice as a public figure, as king. Hector's choice, more unassuming, is a private decision, establishing his freedom as person rather than as official. Besides, Hal could not know the outcome of Agincourt so clearly as Hector knows that Troy will fall in time. Thus the gap between the intellectual and the moral is not so yawning in Hal's case. Troy's future is foreordained, whereas Hal has the advantage of making his own kind of Pascalian wager. The wager is not available to Hector, who knows that he is subject to the fatality of history.

That is, he knows that he is not free insofar as he is a

creature caught in the chronicle of wasting time, which of itself has no human meaning. So he must give his own human meaning to time, and find his identity in time by choosing to act as if he were free to determine his future. This gesture of freedom springs from absurdity, for as Camus remarks, "All great deeds and all great thoughts have a ridiculous beginning"—ridiculous because the gestures that establish our freedom belie the knowledge of our bondage.[7] To use Camus's phrasing, as moral beings we are bound to the postulate of freedom. This postulate is accepted when "starting from a philosophy of the world's lack of meaning, it ends up by finding a meaning and depth in it."

Choosing to behave as if he were free to save Troy from its fate, Hector is in something like our modern position. We have every reason to suspect that some day some madman will press the button to bring about the final solution. To capitulate to this foreknowledge is to submit, rationally enough, to inevitability; but we cease to be men if we behave as if we are not free to choose. So we choose as if we had some choice; we resist. As Camus says, "The mind, when it reaches its limits, must make a judgment and choose its conclusions." Or again to quote Paul Valéry, civilization (as distinct from mere history) is based upon a "fiduciary structure." By this token, Hector is a civilized man, since he is the one who plays the role of acting as if his belief were to be justified by future events. He is, in short, an absurdist. As moral being, he is generating the human value of freedom within the inevitabilities of a situation in which he is bound: *ex nihilo ens fit*—he is creating his being from nothingness by choosing his death.

Neither Troilus nor Paris nor Ulysses with his canniness in exploiting time has this absurd heroism. Troilus and Paris through the spell of their own rational illusions can believe in abstractions like honor, but their will to believe is a blind and reckless triumph, a self-deception. Hector must believe in spite of his knowledge and his doubt. Troilus and Paris are free only because they are deluded by their ideas. Hector is free by another kind of resistance, affirming his identity in the teeth of necessity. He has learned to live under the menacing jurisdiction of time by resisting the dictates of time. Camus defines this paradox: "Assured of his temporally limited freedom, of his revolt devoid of future, and of his mortal consciousness, he lives out his adventure within the span of his lifetime." Freud had reason to say that time is the field in which the ego works, and it has been said that in Shakespeare "value is a function of time."[8]

Hector acts on a faith that is not so much a faith as a conviction, a conviction held against doubts. Neither Troilus nor Paris can doubt. They cannot afford to doubt, which means, in effect, that they have no choice. But Hector says that "modest doubt" is "the beacon of the wise." Troilus and Paris live by their certainties; Hector exists more precariously, prone to examine the causes to which he is committed. He lacks Ulysses's assurance, for Ulysses is at ease because he feels able to exploit the occasion. History is not problematic to Ulysses since he cannot fear.

Though his determination is unwavering, Hector at first takes a tentative position:

> Though no man lesser fears the Greeks than I . . .
> There is no lady of more softer bowels,
> More spongy to suck in the sense of fear,
> More ready to cry out "Who knows what follows?"
> Than Hector is. (II, 2)

Having such misgivings, Hector cannot trust his reason, although he brings reason to bear upon the decision whether to keep Helen. Troilus and Paris, with their irrational rationalism, are assured that in the name of honor they must keep Helen, wiping out the disgrace of her rape by their ability to hold her. They argue that to bring reason to bear upon their decision would invite doubt about their honorable cause: "Reason and respect/ Make livers pale and lustihood deject."

Hector, who is amenable to reason up to the limits of reason, protests that the value of things must be partly affirmed by their worth in themselves, not entirely upon the esteem in which they are held. This sounds like Ulysses' pragmatism, but Hector is simply asking that the judgment made by the mind have some relation to the thing judged. That is, the mind must be brought into some tenable adjustment with what exists outside the mind, otherwise the world becomes a mere construct of the will. "Is your blood so madly hot," Hector asks,

> . . . that no discourse of reason,
> Nor fear of bad success in a bad cause,
> Can qualify the same? (II, 2)

So to stand wilfully is to yield to the passions, not

> . . . to make up a free determination
> 'Twixt right and wrong. . . .
> . . . Thus to persist
> In doing wrong extenuates not wrong,
> But makes it much more heavy. (II, 2)

Thus Hector's moral position is to ask for the considered choice, which he calls "election." For Hector the essence of freedom is a choice made among possibilities fully appraised, and this choice cannot be made by the sanctions of power or utility or abstractions like honor. Choice must be made according to certain moral imperatives, which in Hector's case means losing his life in a cause destined to fail. Since he is a Trojan, he does his duty as a Trojan, though he knows that Troy is doomed and has full recognition that the Trojan cause is dubious.

So much seems clear. But in this play, where all positions seem untenable, one of the most disturbing abandonments comes in Hector's speech at the close of the debate on values when he says, in a tone that rings out of key with his character as elsewhere established:

> . . . yet ne'ertheless,
> My spritely brethren, I propend to you
> In resolution to keep Helen still. (II, 2)

Is Hector being scornful? Condescending? Jocular? Is it possible to read this passage as Hector's (inadequately phrased) affirmation that his "resolution" or choice is to continue acting as a Trojan simply because he will not be an Achilles and sulk? Anyhow, the bantering tone is disconcerting, for Hector is not a bantering person.

The fact, howbeit, remains that in spite of this disquieting tone Hector has played the role of "loyal opposition" (to use the British category) and has throughout the debate brought to bear moral judgments, as his "spritely brethren" do not. However absurd his position, it is the only one by which he can resist injurious time. And his freedom has no meaning apart from these inevitabilities. For Hector the problem of "freedom as such" has no meaning, since his freedom must be found in commitment: "You know me dutiful." Hector, like Sisyphus, has found his burden, his obligation to Troy and to a policy he disapproves. His commitment is a function of his doubt.

In his knowledge and resistance Hector is in many ways closer to Socrates than to Sisyphus—to the Socrates who absurdly accepted the penalties of an Athenian law he disapproved. Hector's position is one of the most difficult to occupy; he is sceptical as Socrates was sceptical. Socrates doubted the justice and validity of Athenian law, but he drank the hemlock. Paul Elmer Moore once mentioned how Socrates absurdly united intellectual scepticism with moral affirmation. So too Rieux and Tarrou in *The Plague* doubt the integrity of the men about them, but they both act as if these men were worth healing, or could be healed.

None of these figures is in a secure or powerful enough position to master the fate assigned them, though they behave as if they were. Like Hector, they are all victims of time but find their identity, their humanity, in resisting time.

Hector lives in a time that makes his freedom both unreal and real. Troy will fall, yet Hector will behave as if Troy were not to fall. Such is the free determination of modern man, an evidence of the peculiar and irrational nature of human freedom, which is both actual and suppositional, as, perhaps, it was in Greek tragedy. So modern man as an individual must believe that he is free to make history even while history victimizes him. Rationally modern man thinks of himself as predestined; morally and politically, he must believe that he is free—a limited and ironic or reduced heroism. Intellectual and moral perceptions are at odds. Hector exists between the reality of the present choice and the certainty of a final outcome. From the standpoint of the onlooker he is predestined; from his personal standpoint he must act as if he were not.[9] His freedom is both actual and illusory. He is free at the moment, like the particle in a Brownian movement, but, also like this particle, ultimately conditioned. He does, and he does not, make his life. But he is responsible for the life that he makes.

Ulysses, with his talent for exploiting the occasion, is free in a more superficial sense, for he does not choose with Hector's consciousness of the futility of his choice. Troilus and Paris are free in a still more unreal sense, for they are deceived by their own egoistic command of their world; their heroism and honor are empty of human value. Cressida is the only one besides Hector who exists under the threat of human time, though she does not have Hector's freedom because her commitment to the moment is an act of despair instead of a rebellion against time.

Hector stands as the only victim of time who is not destroyed by time. He has learned the meaning of dreadful freedom inflicted upon him by the collapse of a world order where a hierarchical system designated responsibilities but minimized choice, the choice that is an index to the quality of selfhood, though in the long course of time it is irrelevant and only an aspect of fatality. Hector's life is a model of the ethical experience of new western man born with the Renaissance into a condition of superfluous but necessary heroism. His freedom is a contingency, but a contingency that secures his position in a world order where contingency has merely a statistical value. Duty, chosen as a gesture against time, is a commitment made only in the face of doubt but marking a height of consciousness.

VIII
The Extremity of Time:
Lear

At the end of the play Lear cries, "Howl, howl, howl," then poses the unanswerable question, "Why should a dog, a horse, a rat have life/ And thou no breath at all?" Faced with such a query, how can we say that Lear has learned something salutary or that ripeness is all? For *Lear* is a *Blick ins Chaos,* or what Jan Kott has called "the decay and fall of the world." It is testimony to the modernity of Shakespeare that this play anticipates the fascination of recent literature with the terrifying silence that sets in when we have discovered that we can say nothing truly intelligible about our world. As Samuel Beckett puts it: ". . . for the likes of us and no matter how we are recounted there is more nourishment in a cry nay a sigh torn from one whose only good is silence or in speech extorted from one at last delivered from its use than sardines can ever offer." *(How It Is)* In *Lear,* "nothing will come of nothing," and in this play, "the quality of nothing," as Gloucester says, does not "hide itself." Here Shakespeare seems to have accepted Beckett's principle (Democritean) that "nothing is more real than nothing."

Lear's course is an unbearable purgatorial discipline without apparent final redemption, an inversion of Dante's *ascent,* a spectacle of anguish nearly gratuitous, and a foreshadowing of Antonin Artaud's theatre of cruelty. The descent is not really into hell, for hell is a domain where penalty is exacted on some principle of justice. But Lear's question why a rat should have life and Cordelia none confirms that there is no operative justice. Lear has passed across the border of meaning into a frightening, inscrutable nihilism of nonmeaning, the far side of zero; or, to use language that is current, into the area of noninformation. If the usual tragic action phrases, or "codes," a logic of human experience, *Lear* gives us no information that can be coded, except in the Gloucester subplot.

I am deliberately using the language of information theory, for once again we have an illustration of Shakespeare's uncanny prescience about ideas that were not formulated until more than three centuries after his death. Just as *Hamlet* and *Measure for Measure* intuit certain psychoanalytic theories, *Lear* has an almost startling relevance to recent information theory and testifies to Shakespeare's ability to feel the future on the instant.

Without pretending to have mastered the science of cybernetics, the layman can grasp those features of information theory that apply to the abnormalities of *Lear*.[1] Information is what can be communicated by being coded, and whatever the code being used (words, line, color, symbols, numbers), the coding must, at least to some extent, exclude what is called "noise," that is, the signals that are extraneous to the code being used. Noise is noninformation, that which intrudes from the background to confuse or "strangulate" the message being conveyed by the code.

The irony is that the more sensitive the transmitter, the more noise it is liable to pick up as "interference" or "nonmeaning" which obstructs or obscures the information being transmitted. For example, the telegraph with its simple coding of clicks will transmit information without ambiguity even if a freight train is passing while the message is being transmitted. By contrast, a sensitive stereophonic

mechanism will pick up background noise from other elec-
tronic devices, noise that confuses the message. In short,
the narrow band width of telegraphic coding successfully
excludes what is not being coded, though the message is
simplistically phrased. By the same token, a poem by Edgar
Guest "comes through" clearly and precisely because the
coding has a narrow band width. Yet a poem like "Lycidas," with its much wider band width, its delicate receptive
mechanism, is always in danger of picking up a great deal
of "background noise" which "interferes" with the trans-
mission. Thus "Lycidas" is vulnerable to "misunderstanding" as a poem by Guest is not.

But it is exactly this danger of misunderstanding that
validates the range of what is being coded. Thus too the
simple coding of the revenger's plot in *Hamlet* is obscured,
if not confused, by the contaminations of a very wide range
of psychic "noise." *Hamlet* is a play that picks up "interruptions" and "interferences." T. S. Eliot is correct in saying
that *Hamlet* is an "artistic failure" if by artistic success we
mean coding that is crystal clear, without this interference.
The reply to Eliot's point is in Robert Penn Warren's essay
on "Pure and Impure Poetry," "Poetry wants to be pure,
but poems do not," and some of the most effective poems
are filled with ambiguities that result from the infiltration
of background noise.

Consequently the question rephrases itself: how much
background noise can a work of art tolerate or accommodate? The well-made play or the "poem" that is coded simply by plot, rhyme, metre, and platitudes accurately and
directly conveys its meaning by excluding intimations, ambiguities, and "impurities" that are not caught in its narrow band width.[2] The more embracing the experience, the
more it is susceptible to interference, unintelligibility, and
the strangulation of a clear "message." The drag toward
nonmeaning or noise operates in the tension between or-
der/disorder in Michaelangelo's last sculptures, where the

"form" emerges from a formlessness but tends to sink back into the formless. These sculptures are among the most disturbing spectacles in the arts, an exercise (sometimes like Goya's nightmarish visions) in the limits of nihilism in artistic vision. The modern sensitivity to nonmeanings in our existence is expressed in Robbe-Grillet's novels and "chosiste" art. The key word in Robbe-Grillet's fiction and film is *peut-être*, perhaps.

Lear has the widest band width of any Shakespearean action because it more than others accommodates "non-meaning" by picking up an extraordinary range of background noise, the nihilistic meaninglessness that cannot be coded, the chaos and old night behind creation. This is a matter that has concerned Gestalt psychologists. E. H. Gombrich has raised the question to what extent a "good Gestalt" is necessary to painting. The good Gestalt (or, more accurately, *Praegnanz*) is a means of coding, and Anton Ehrenzweig in *The Hidden Order of Art* has extended his thesis advanced in his earlier book on *The Psycho-Analysis of Artistic Vision and Hearing*, proposing that the most potent artistic statements have a strong tension between Gestalt and non-Gestalt vision, the latter called "peripheral" or "low-level" vision.

In this low-level or eiditic vision the child is able to see the "figure" and the "ground" together, that is, to hold the Gestalt and the non-Gestalt in the same focus. Only later, when the child learns (or is taught) to isolate the Gestalt, does this ambiguous or "double" vision disappear, or become repressed, so that he seeks out the "form" of the object without including the formless background in the same focus. Note that Ehrenzweig is not arguing that the background non-Gestalt is more important than the Gestalt, but only that a narrow coding of vision overemphasizes the Gestalt at the expense of the non-Gestalt perceptions. The vision of a great painter or poet remains "polyphonic" by counterpointing the background "form-

lessness" against the foreground figure imposed and organized by the conscious mind.

Thus the sensitivity of a major artist allows the non-
Gestalt noise to impinge upon, or intrude into, his coding.
Milton cannot entirely code "Lycidas" in the classical, pa-
gan, and pastoral Gestalt, and this great poem remains, in
John Crowe Ransom's helpful phrase, almost anonymous
in its radical impurity, its "illegitimate" implications, for
the background noise (Milton's undisciplined egoism, his
puritanism, his half-repressed ambition) interferes with its
traditional form, giving the poem a disturbance that is not
fully controlled. The poem resounds with infiltrations
from the unconscious.

This background or non-Gestalt infiltration—impure,
uncoded, or "meaningless"—is an aspect of the ultimate
noise or nonmeaning that science links with entropy. In a
state of complete entropy no pattern or coding is possible,
since there is a final distribution or leveling of energy that
has "run down" to zero. This zero degree or final equilibrium is an extreme nihilism or ultimate "meaninglessness."
Thus the "noise" that erodes distinct or encoded information is entropic. Codings with a wide band width are most
susceptible to this entropic eroding.

The intrusion of the non-Gestalt or "formless" is a danger in the arts corresponding to the second law of thermodynamics. According to this law heat diffuses from hotter
to colder bodies until there is a leveling of energy that
obliterates all differences and results in the death of the
system. What we call life is a transient resistance to, or
suspension of, entropy, which in its last form we call death,
the stability of nothingness. Vitality is low entropy (negentropy), but the wider its band width—the more sensitive it
is to background noise—the less it can be coded in any clear
Gestalt. Entropy, in brief, is the ultimate nihilism.

Lear is an exercise in the limits of nihilism in drama, a
breakthrough of nonmeaning. The Gloucester plot is sup-

posed to be parallel to the Lear plot, but this proves not to be the case except superficially. The Gloucester plot is close to the conventional formula (or coding) of tragic action, in which an error is retributed by some disaster befalling him who blundered. By contrast the Lear plot, a crawling to-ward death, is an eruption of entropic noise that can be expressed only in a howl, the cry of one who has felt the meaninglessness of life. The Gloucester plot makes "sense." The Lear plot gravitates toward that horrible final question why a rat should have life and Cordelia not.

Lear is an alarming representation of the Gestalt and non-Gestalt held, ruthlessly, in the same focus, creating tensions that are as unendurable as those in Michaelan-gelo's last sculptures, which are not "unfinished" but mon-strous apparitions from a background nothingness. If life is resistance to entropy, then Goneril, Regan, Edmund are most "alive"; their aggression confines their existence to the narrowest band width, excluding all sensitivity to the background noise that strangulates meaning in Lear's expe-rience. Goneril, Regan, Edmund know all too well what life "means." Their coding is simplistic, legible. But Lear hears the background noise of noninformation—or mad-ness. Here the "meaningless" takes on "meaning."

Among modern philosophers Heidegger has adopted the idea of entropy by interpreting life as a being that arises from nothingness, an *exstasis* or "standing out" against the final horizon of nonbeing, which is death. As an episode in negentropy, life is what Thomas Mann called it, a strange fever that runs in matter. Biologically the emergence of species is a form of coding, but the appearance of the indi-vidual with his own "personality" is an even stranger case of coded information.

Yet so far as the entire universe is concerned, entropy appears to operate, and in the case of the person entropy reappears, as Heidegger suggests, in our progress toward death, which is an entropic destiny for each. Although our life is an assertion of negentropy, entropy becomes a feature of that life through the process of ageing and extinction. According to the old proverb we begin to die as soon as we are born. Freud defined life as the course by which we choose our way to death. Therefore in spite of the momentary suspension of entropy, the second law of thermodynamics is relevant so far as the person is concerned. The physicist phrases the situation by saying, "Changes in any isolated system always occur in a way such that the entropy of the system increases or, at the least, remains constant."[3]

This increase in entropy in the isolated system—the life of the person—bears upon the nature of human time. Regardless of the uncertainty about any possible reversibility of time, it still seems true that the direction of time in our universe is indicated by an increase in entropy. In a universe where time schemes have become relative, the theory of entropy affords a usable measure, for the rate and direction of time can be indicated on a scale down which any system runs toward its extinction. This gain in entropy is the flight of "time's arrow," a unidirectional flow that is not symbolized by clock or chronometric time. Entropic time is the running down of the system into a condition in which energy is so leveled or dissipated that all distinctions disappear when a state of absolute zero is reached, a nothingness that is a final cosmic absurdity, a condition that cannot be coded because no information is available. Or, to quote *Lear*, "Nothing will come of nothing." *Ex nihilo, nihil fit.* In such a condition nothing can be said. At this ultimate horizon of "noise" we reach the limits of nihilism, an "O without a figure," to quote the Fool.

The time problem in *Lear* inheres in this gravitation toward nothingness, this flow of "natural" time, giving it direction. But there is another way of giving direction to time, that is, coding it by a logic of causality: if we do A, then B follows, and if we do B, then C follows. The logic of causality gives time a direction, and without such a logic we find it difficult (as Hume and Kant said) to encode experience. Lacking such a code, existence becomes nonsense. In the *Lear* world there is a serious dislocation of this logical coding. There is no coherent or intelligible "earlier-to-later course," no unidirectional past-to-future flow of time. In this hideously anachronistic world—different from the world of *Macbeth* or the vertical experience of time in *Hamlet* or the compulsive time in *Othello* or the anxiety to arrest time in *Love's Labour's Lost* or the pacific time in *Antony and Cleopatra*—old fools are babes again. In *Lear* time is more seriously out of joint than in any Shakespearean play.

Here time is nonsense. To perceive why this is so, we may quote Richard Schlegel, who describes two different situations in which time cannot be coded:

> Conceivably the world could be so featureless as to have no natural change by which one state of the universe could be distinguished from any other; in such a quiet world, there would be no basis for a concept of time, for there would be no way of establishing time differences. At the other extreme, the world might be in so chaotic a state of continual change that there would be no regularity by which a time scale, or measure of time, could be established.[4]

This statement is a key to *Lear*. In the latter world events would happen meaninglessly in a disorder that would be unintelligible noise. In the former world nothing would happen at all, for there would be complete entropy, a state of noninformation or total silence.

Lear has both sorts of meaninglessness. First, there is the unintelligible noise of complete disorder. Then there is the final quiet world of death, which is an entropic condition in which nothing happens. The noise of the unintelligible disorder which breaks through all codings marks Lear's experience with his daughters; then follows the ultimate silence of a final nothingness which is not only death but

a total equilbrium of a peace passing all understanding—
a noise that is eternal silence.

To take the chaotic noise first, Lear's experience with
Goneril and Regan is an index to the nonsense or noninformation where time is out of joint, time lacking any unidirectional flow, any logical sequence. There is a strange and
unresolved conflict between the mad rapidity with which
events happen and the agonizing waiting. Under this sud-
denness, when events happen "all at once,"[5] any temporal
or causal coding becomes impossible, for fecundity means
not a succession of generations but the young displacing
the old out of season. Lear refers to the illogicality of this
situation by asking, "Is there any cause in nature that
makes these hard hearts?"

Perhaps not enough has been made of the haste of the
Lear action, which is a disruption of time and a perversion
of any scale by which to make sense of experience. In a
searching phrase Blake called time the mercy of eternity,
for it may be the only way man can carry the affliction and
the fear by encoding his history. But history requires some
sequential order, some logic of cause and effect. Neither
appears in Lear's experience, which has an exponential
acceleration of time. Edgar is the only one who waits out
his time. At the beginning Lear wilfully disorients the time
scheme by his rashness, as if he were not old. The action
opens so abruptly that there is no psychological or rational
context for his disastrous blunder.

Lear has usurped his life within the first 250 lines of the
play. The time scheme of the conventional plot is violently
distorted; there is no "rising action," for the play opens
with a crisis so steep that the remainder is a relentless
peripeteia in reckless tempo, a protracted and agonizing *dénouement,* a descent into a purgatory from which there is no
exit. The King of France cannot understand why Cordelia,
Lear's "best and dearest," should in "a trice of time" be
dismantled of all favor. The Fool comprehends this irra-

tional exclusion of the gradual, genetic course of time, charging Lear with making his daughters his mothers: "Then they for sudden joy did weep." Lear demands instantaneous service: "Let me not stay a jot for dinner; go get it ready." Regan visits Cornwall "out of season," and Oswald as "a reeking post, Stewed in his haste," appears "half breathless" to deliver letters "spite of intermission." With the same mad rapidity Lear's daughters strip him of his hundred knights, at a stroke reducing them to twenty-five, to ten, to five, to none. Then the tempest breaks like "thought-executing fires"; France is "so suddenly gone back," and Albany prays that the heavens "send quickly down" spirits to tame these offences.

Maynard Mack has made the point that the action lacks any "psychological antecedents." The foreshortened psychology in *Lear* is a symptom of a chaotic time scheme. Motives manifest themselves only during the course of time, and the whole play is one of lost time, the events happening in a frantic disjunction, cancelling out the intervals during which motives could generate and change. Hence the absurdist psychology that makes the old infantile again, an anti-psychology culminating in Edmund's preposterous final reversal: "Some good I mean to do/ Despite of mine own nature." The lack of any progressive time results in a nonlogic of unmediated extremes. The headlong ellipsis of Lear's calamity gives the play a strangely warped design, as if it were validation of a thesis that did not need to be developed but only posited, as if we knew the conclusion before going through the proof.

And behind all this haste is the slow, agonizing endurance, changeless, stretching Lear on the rack of the world, the waiting that is so Kafka-like in a state where nothing mitigates the cruelty, the pitiless horror that makes man an unaccommodated forked animal who learns nothing except the art of his necessities. Stranger than all is Edgar's remark that ripeness is all, a sentiment that makes no sense whatever amid this chaos, except, perhaps, that since nothing can change, man must endure everything. For nothing changes in the Lear world; the disorder is uniform and monotonous, making all distinction in suffering noninformation.

The ellipsis in time means a breakdown in causality, a breakdown that implies absurdity. It is disturbingly abnormal that Lear's woes arise from trusting his daughters, his supposing that "future strife may be prevented now" by committing his power to those who love him most. Gloucester's speech on the late eclipses of sun and moon indicate how the code of cause and effect has ruptured, though man "can reason it thus and thus," the wisdom of nature does not help, and man is "scourged by the sequent effects." Gloucester's despair is like a satire on the Baconian optimism that if we understand causes and effects, we can make nature a handmaiden for man's use and satisfaction.

In the Lear world all human codes are irrelevant, for brothers divide, bonds between father and child are cracked, and ruinous disorders follow us to the grave. So, as the Fool sings, out went the candle and we are left darkling in an era when the hedge sparrow feeds the cuckoo only to have its head bit off. The Fool sees the meaninglessness of the noninformation in this world. The breakdown of every code is best phrased in the Fool's song proposing that whether we behave well or ill, England is a chaos either way. When priests are more in word than matter and nobles are their tailors' tutors *or* when every case in law is right and slanders do not live in tongues, then the realm comes to great confusion. It makes no difference. The old are not wise; a daughter is a disease in the flesh; age is unnecessary.

As in Hardy's *Jude the Obscure*, there is no answer. The play poses the mystery mentioned by Miranda in *The Tempest*: good wombs bear bad sons. *Lear* is Shakespeare's most rigorous inquisition into the unaccountable existence of

evil, which is the radical noise at the heart of existence. The
play is an eruption of "interferences"; its band width is so
wide that these grim interferences confuse every coding
capable of giving an intelligible message.

In *Lear*, life itself is a vicious form of negentropy, an
upheaval of a chaos that cannot be coded morally or rationally. Life is combat. The preface to *Lear* was Ulysses'
speech on disorder in *Troilus and Cressida*. Ulysses urges
that without the social and personal code of degree, priority, and place there are only discord and oppugnancy: force
overwhelms justice, and power, activated by will and appetite,

> Must make perforce an universal prey,
> And last eat up himself. (I, 3)

Life, which should be man's coding of the nothingness
from which he emerges, here becomes a decoding, a version
of noninformation and disorder—not the featureless entropic quiet that is the final background noise. Total meaninglessness might be consoling, but the meaninglessness of
Lear's experience is unbearable. Noise becomes discord,
not rest. So Kent speaks, properly enough, the suitable
epitaph for the dead Lear: Do not stretch him longer on the
rack of his world. The "high noises" to which Edgar refers
(the meaning of the phrase has been debated) are interferences that vibrate again in our modern drama, our theatre
of cruelty explored by Antonin Artaud, a theatre that
Hardy visited in *Jude*.

These noises were also heard by Freud when he wrote
his grimmest essay on "Instincts and Their Vicissitudes,"
which is another preface to *Lear*. Freud suggested that the
primal relation of the self to objects is hate rather than love,
for the drive toward entropy in the self is such that it does
not wish to be disturbed; it seeks its fullest pleasure in that
total peace we call death. Since stimuli impinging from the
outside world agitate the self, it seeks to reject or even

destroy whatever causes it unrest. If life, or negentropy, is
a response to stimuli from without, then life is primarily
a rejection of whatever disturbs our narcissistic tranquil-
lity. Thus hate is older than love, and more instinctive. *Lear*
extends this Freudian thesis beyond its limits, for here the
course of maturing is one of intensifying hate. Edgar has
this nihilistic interpretation of life and time when he exclaims:

> . . . World, world, O world!
> But that thy strange mutations make us hate thee
> Life would not yield to age. (IV, 1)

By this canon Goneril and Regan are mature, and Lear's
age is not ripeness but an extreme of hate which has become the mark of his character: he rejects Cordelia with the
barbarity of a Scythian. If life is a suspension of entropy,
then Lear's negentropy affirms itself by a hate that has led
him to reject a daughter who has disturbed his narcissism.
Lear reverses the situation in *Othello,* where love is primary
and the corruption of love is a cause for hate. From a
Freudian view time is out of joint in *Lear,* for if the primal
response in life is hate, then indeed old fools are babes
again. *Lear* may be the only Shakespearean play where the
abiding meaning of vitality is aggression. Lear is mad, or
at least deluded; but the appalling fact is that hate is embod-
ied in the effectual characters—Goneril, Regan, Edmund,
Cornwall. The forgiving, loving Cordelia, like the Fool, is
helpless, merely ancillary to the savages who at last destroy
themselves by their ruthless sanity. Even Gloucester learns
to hate.

In other words, *Lear* moves "beyond culture" and belongs in the theatre of cruelty. Artaud intended to create
a drama that is anticultural, beyond codes, revealing the
nihilism of a dark background catastrophe showing that
the sky can fall on our heads. He wanted to move "beyond
psychology" by presenting a convulsion behind our false

culture. Artaud hoped to bare the danger in a reality "behind our reality," a condition where flesh is blooded under the hammer or extirpated with knives—a theatre of the block, the gibbet, the crematorium, or madhouse. He holds that "all clear ideas are dead ideas," and he aims at a dissociation through manic laughter. "We must have done with psychology," he states, by touching a future that is disaster. "Everything that cannot be expressed by words must be brought into the foreground." There is Lear's final howl. Thus, according to Artaud, theatre must move beyond the text.

For Artaud, theatrical action should be a persecution that is fatal, with destruction used as a transforming force, a "voracious" anarchy releasing conflicts at the limit of a "vertigo" not to be controlled and a "disorder verging on chaos." And *Lear* is a choral spectacle, a tumult of mighty discords. In this theatre we cringe at the "noise" beyond our codes, since the mark of our epoch is confusion. Shakespeare projected this play into extragalactic spaces, an abyss where life is convulsive and time is multidirectional.

Lear inverts the existential principle that life is an apparition of being from nothingness, a coding or figure that arises from the negative background of entropic "distribution" or leveling of energy. In *Lear* this emergence is *also* a disorder, the unintelligible noise of a world where there is no morality but only authority, a frenzy causing her father to curse Goneril, hoping that her organs of increase will so shrivel that if she teem at all she will mother a child to torment her. The cancellation of all human codes means that *Lear* has reached the limits of nihilism, negating the normal logic of tragedy by which there is some penalty for a mistake committed by one who is inherently great and good.

Lear made a ghastly blunder in alienating his power to Goneril and Regan, but it is hard to say that he is inherently great and good. He is mad at the start and mad at the end and mad in the intervening period. For this play is unremitting mania, and Lear speaks truly when he says that he is old and not in his right mind. Thus he moves into the spectrum of the clinical rather than the tragic. Psychology tells us that madness is the hidden ground, the background noise, behind reason. The uncoded noise disrupts the coding, strangulating meaning. This action is a savage rebellion against reason, so that at last Lear is driven to ask why a rat should have life and Cordelia not. Lear suffers the afflictions of Job, but this drama has no Jehovah. It is nearly a parody of Calvinist autocratic divine dispensation, without grace extended.

Yet the tragic figure has not entirely disappeared against the background noise, for there is the subplot or pattern of Gloucester's experience, which makes better tragic sense. Gloucester is not of great stature, but he is not mad. He is a casual and well-disposed man, too careless in his sexual life and heedless of convention. Unlike Lear, he is magnanimous enough to acknowledge and cherish Edmund his bastard. He blunders, then pays a dreadful penalty. Gloucester's course yields intelligible "information" as Lear's does not, and Edgar encodes an almost Sophoclean "message" that comes through without distortion or interference when he tells Edmund of his father's fate:

> The gods are just, and of our pleasant vices
> Make instruments to plague us.
> The dark and vicious place where thee he got
> Cost him his eyes. (V, 3)

This imposed penalty has a tragic logic missing in Lear's appraisal of his own condition:

> You do me wrong to take me out 'o th' grave.
> Thou art a soul in bliss; but I am bound
> Upon a wheel of fire, that mine own tears
> Do scald like molten lead. (IV, 7)

If there are limits to the nihilism in *Lear*, they are set not in the major action, culminating in "Never, never, never," but, instead, in the Gloucester subplot, which is structurally but not morally parallel to the major plot. Structurally, the Gloucester plot does in *Lear* what the revenger's plot does in *Hamlet*, it serves as a "figure" to counterpoint the uncoded "ground," and affirms that life is subject to an ethic of retribution.

One of the reassuring themes in the lightning-like excesses of *Lear* is the need for "distribution." The term takes on two distinguishable meanings, the less obvious being the necessity of some mean or degree of moderation between extremes. This ideal of the golden mean is, in effect, a form of ethical coding or "information," a moral imperative that has a long history in western thought from Plato's quest for temperance onward. Only by such a code can man cope with his otherwise nihilistic impulses. The tragic code of retribution manifest in the Gloucester action springs from a conviction that a blunder or wrong choice is visited by some penalty to right the balance.

But so far as the Lear action goes, this code is annulled, since all choices seem absurd or meaningless in this anarchic world; they all lead to nothing. Lear is responsible for the first of the absurd choices when he offers Cordelia to Burgundy and France by a logic of the excluded middle: will they have her, honest as she is, without any dowry except his curse, or will they have her with dowry but dishonest? Burgundy makes the proper reply: "Election makes not up on such conditions." Edmund offers us the same kind of choice of extremes that negate each other: which is to be preferred, a legitimate son who is a fop begot passionlessly between stale, tired sheets, or a vigorous illegitimate son begot with passion? By excluding the middle (the legitimate son begot with passion, or the illegitimate fop begot without passion), the alternatives become fallacious. The same kind of excluded middle reappears in Hardy's novels, where the only valid sexuality is extralegal.

The mutilated logic of the excluded middle is inherent in Goneril's opinion that old fools are babes again. There is no such thing, so far as Lear himself goes, as a wise old man. Lear, like Gloucester, speaks of the absurdity of extremes, which are the only choices offered. When Lear is deprived of all his followers, he pleads that even a beggar is "in the poorest thing superfluous," having something more than nature needs. And Gloucester phrases the absurdity in this world when he appeals to the heavens to chasten the lust-dieted man

> So distribution should undo excess,
> And each man have enough. (IV, 1)

This second and obvious need for distribution is phrased also by Lear when he finds himself a naked wretch, an unaccommodated forked animal deprived of everything in the storm:

> . . . Take physic, pomp;
> Expose thyself to feel what wretches feel,
> That thou mayst shake the superflux to them
> And show the heavens more just. (III, 4)

So the Lear world lacks the distribution that enables man to endure his life. The unmediated extremes in *Lear* are nonsensical, obliterating any ethical measure, offering no index of maturity, justice, or the possibility of encoding experience or time. The noninformation of the Lear world, with its deformed logic or suspension of logic, results in a kind of identity of opposites: "The art of our necessities is strange,/ And can make vile things precious." Here is a dialectic that is mad. In the chaos of this world there is a new transvaluing of values, for the most valid of all human experiences seems to be insanity. This is the limit of nihilism, beyond which we cannot go.

To be exact, the limit seems to be reached in Edgar's speech: "The worst is not/ So long as we can say 'This is the worst.'" That is, the worst is reached only when all possibility of comparison is gone in the face of an extremity so utter that judgment no longer operates and the ability to distinguish is completely paralyzed. This is *desperatio*, the condition of those in Dante's hell, where reason is left behind. It is a movement to the very center of evil or negation, like the descent to Satan's navel at the minus pole of things where all values vanish at the axis of an ignorance that is absolute noninformation: total meaninglessness. When we have touched this point, in utter darkness, a final nothingness and nihilism, all responses lose significance in darkest absurdity. At the heart of the Lear torment is only reason in madness.

Nevertheless behind this encounter with absolute absurdity it is possible to read still another meaning of distribution according to the entropy that gives some coherence and direction to time and life. Here the second law of thermodynamics comes into play, for if life is an affirmation of anti-entropy (negentropy) the whole of life heads toward that final distribution which we call death—a distribution that annihilates selfhood and eventually sends us back into the quiet where there is no disturbance, where there is no time. This total quiet is an ultimate chaos to redeem us from that *other* chaos in *Lear*, a state "so featureless" that one condition cannot be distinguished from any other, where there is, in Edgar's phrase, no distinction between worse and worst. Death, which is the manifestation of entropy in human existence, is a peace passing understanding, and we must learn to accept that peace.

If Lear's own experience offers us any encoded information, it arises from the myth that Freud discussed in his early essay on "The Theme of the Three Caskets." According to this myth, man, like Paris, has a choice among three goddesses: Hera, Aphrodite, and Minerva—woman in her three guises as Mother, Lover, and the Wisdom who is our Last Mother or Death, the Ugly One or the Inexorable. Man must learn to choose Atropos, the plainest of the three, as Bassanio learned to choose the leaden casket. The final choice must be "Mutter Erde," the dust to which we return at our last distribution. In this final distribution we undo the excesses of our life, its negentropy or aggression. The bearing upon Lear is betokened by the last scene when he bears lovingly the body of Cordelia, the homely honest one who is redemptive. Lear has learned to choose death, to return to the womb that makes our being seem moments in eternal silence. Wordsworth learned this lesson more easily, without having to endure Lear's wrenching discipline. Instinctively Wordsworth, with wise passivity, chose Lucy, the goddess who represents a final unintelligible peace. No motion has she, no force, having surrendered to the All.

Earlier Lear tried to make Goneril and Regan his mothers, but Cordelia is the Great Mother who is able to bring him peace, the entropic Silence that is finally picked up by a play that until the very end confuses every coding by its discords, the noise that is the violence of a hate and hostility Lear shares with his evil daughters—a discord that makes time meaningless. With its cosmically wide band width, *Lear* catches the interruptions of two kinds of nonmeaning: the rage that cracks nature's molds, and the solacing entropic reduction that is beyond all codes or coding. Until the last, Lear's life is an expression of nihilism, the nihilism first that is injurious, then the nihilism that reaches outside the extremity of time into the timeless.

IX

The Scenic Resolution

In the sixth chapter of the *Poetics* Aristotle identifies the parts of tragedy and goes on to remark that of these "the spectacle *(opsis)*, though an attraction, is the least artistic of all the parts and has the least to do with the art of poetry." The meaning of the term spectacle has been much discussed, but it is prevailing opinion that Aristotle could hardly have meant the full *mise en scène* since the Greek theatre had few technical resources. An accepted modern version of the *opsis* passage reads, "the spectacle is more a matter for the costumier than the poet." That is, the spectacle must refer to the "look of the characters," their make-up and garb. Gerald Else translates, "As for the costuming, it has emotional power to be sure, but is the least artistic element," for "*opsis* brings up the rear," and cannot refer to the staging as a whole. Yet we are told that the appearance of the actors was impressive enough to cause some of the spectators of *The Eumenides* to faint or have miscarriages.

In any case the matter of "scene" should not be quickly dismissed, for whatever *opsis* may imply, Sophocles' *Oedipus in Colonus* has a dramatic effect arising from the atmosphere in the sacred precinct, a grove filled with chthonic voices, the locale to which the aged, wearied King of Thebes retires and in which he undergoes a transfiguration. The

Messenger tells us about this "wonder" when Oedipus
went to the brink of the chasm near the stone tomb "where
the brazen stairway plunges into the roots of the earth."
There was a peal of thunder, "the voice of the God of
Earth; and the women trembled and wept, falling at their
father's knees." Then there was silence until a voice called,
"It is time; you stay too long." Oedipus "heard the sum-
mons and knew it was from a god." When the company had
gone a little aside, in a scene recalling the transfiguration
of Christ or His ascension, "we turned and looked back.
Oedipus was nowhere to be seen. In what manner he
passed away from this earth, no one can tell."

This miracle could have taken place only in the radiant
vale near Athens, a *temenos* where pain and blindness and
the torment of life are at last eased in a scenic harmony that
makes the close of the play so unlike the close of *Lear*. This
episode is "spectacle" in a sense Aristotle does not seem to
have had in mind. After all his anguish Oedipus comes to
a shrine that belongs in a special category of the spectacular:

> . . . this heaven-fostered haunt, earth's fairest home,
> Gleaming Colonus, where the nightingale
> In cool green covert warbles ever clear,
> True to the clustering ivy and the dear
> Divine, impenetrable shade.

Within this tranquil atmosphere the insolence, the defile-
ment, and the wrath and discord are dispelled. There is
resolution by scene. The transformation or transfiguration
of man in Colonus reminds us that the Greeks had a strong
sense of the "holy place," the Locus of the One, the inviolable ground where the oracle could speak. Anciently this
place was marked by the Omphalos, the earth's navel. The
sacred rites at Delphi, with its shrines and pythian voices,
took place near the Omphalos on the awesome slopes of
Parnassus.

Sophocles is, in his own Greek way, as versatile as Shakespeare, and *Oedipus in Colonus* causes a doubt how many lost plays may have been spectacular in this way, making *mise en scène* a climate. The action does not fall within the Aristotelian definition of tragedy any more than does *The Tempest*, another drama in which there is a sea-change of life in a magical environment, an isle with strange noises, sounds, and sweet airs that make even Caliban dream and where there is a similar transformation of man. For as old Gonzalo says, everyone in Prospero's isle is most himself when no man is his own. This transfiguring of man, this suspension of evil and onset of forgiveness, occurs only in a certain landscape.

In *Oedipus in Colonus* and *The Tempest*, then, the locus of the drama is not merely a setting. Setting is an inert theatrical convenience or designation accessory to the action; it is an auxiliary or technical accompaniment rather than a dramatic influence.[1] By contrast, scene is an operative and, in Coleridge's term, an esemplastic or molding influence in determining dramatic conditions and the state of consciousness in characters and audience. Scene is a context for the experience represented. *All's Well That Ends Well*, for example, has multiple settings in Rousillon, Paris, Florence, Marseilles, which could just as well be London, Venice, Mantua, or Orleans as far as the experience goes. But it would be hard to excerpt the action of *Hamlet* from its atmosphere, the rotten state of Denmark, which affords a tenor of malaise, treachery, ambiguity disturbing the behavior of all the personages. Hamlet is scenic in that it could not take place in another psychological climate. Elsinore is more than mere place. The fifth act, especially, is permeated by the tonality of the graveyard. As C. S. Lewis says, the play is "about" death. In *Macbeth* too there is a darkness which is not mere "setting," but a psychic increment.

The submergence of action in an atmosphere is one of

the "hidden orders of art" (to use Anton Ehrenzweig's phrase), a kind of "unconscious integration" or temper where the scenographic becomes a psychography, not simply a geographic locality. There appears the "oceanic" quality of which Freud spoke, a quality that appears in Wordsworth's ability to grasp "the whole of nature as involved in the tonality of the particular instance," as Whitehead noted. Coleridge must have felt this in Wordsworth, and speaks of the poet as diffusing "a tone and spirit of unity, that blends and (as it were) *fuses,* each into each, by that synthetic and magical power, to which we have exclusively appropriated the name of Imagination." And Baudelaire remarked that by its tone a painting inhabits its own atmosphere, like a dream.

It is frequently supposed that the changes in Shakespeare's later plays can be attributed, as in *The Tempest* or *Cymbeline* or *Winter's Tale,* to the theatrical resources of the indoor theatre and the mechanisms of the masque. But this change is ultimately not attributable to *mise en scène;* it is a question of poetic drama, a peculiar kind of environmental theatre where space is transvalued to atmosphere. Gaston Roupnel in his *Nouvelle Siloë* refers to such a transformation when he says that mathematical or geometric space is a lie, whereas atmospheric space is not. Atmospheric space cannot be fragmented into isolated areas or local passages; it embraces and penetrates by means of a psychic ecology.

Hitherto we have been concerned with the theme that in Shakespearean drama "time is the vehicle of freedom and value."[2] Yet there is a sense in which Shakespeare uses space too as a vehicle of freedom and value. But it is not space as ordinarily conceived, or at least as the Renaissance often conceived it in mathematics and painting. Space is not necessarily environment, as we find in tracing the history of Renaissance art, which used space in two distinguishable ways. There was the treatment of space by ocular perspective or foreshortening, which geometrized space

and gave it a rational coherence lacking in medieval painting, where the gold background is a spiritual environment,
an embracing light. Closely affiliated with logic and Merca-
tor projection, Renaissance space was a geometry of closure, system, demonstration, the *certezze* that finally culmi-
nates in the spatial definition of the Newtonian world
view.

This geometric space makes man an observer, for perspective required the fabrication of an artificial world on a
two-dimensional surface from which the beholder was excluded by a window view of reality. Such mathematized
space is not necessarily environmental space or atmosphere
and it leads toward an entirely rational coherence. Kenneth
Clark comments on how "about the year 1420 some change
in the action of the human mind demanded a new nexus of
unity, enclosed space. In a very extended sense of the term,
this new way of thinking about the world may be called
scientific, for it involved the sense of relation and comparison, as well as the measurement on which science is based."

The other kind of Renaissance space, which might be
called poetic instead of scientific, appears in Leonardo's
blue distances, creating an atmosphere that transforms art
to a version of dream. Kenneth Clark associates this kind
of painting with the Renaissance fantastic landscape, over
which falls a strange light, so that Altdorfer, for instance,
transformed his landscape into a new world. Sir Kenneth
remarks that such landscapes have a relation to quietism,
which is suggested by the Leonardo blue distance. This
sort of atmospheric space was established by Shakespeare
before his company moved to their indoor theatre. At the
close of *Midsummer Night's Dream* Puck dismisses the audience with his admonition that they have but slumbered
here while watching shadows. And Theseus has his own
quietist vision of things, almost like Prospero.

The poetic space or vision of the fantastic landscape is
also a vehicle of freedom, and it has always been inherent

in what Ruskin called the "landscape instinct," which has a continuous history in the arts. It produced pastoral in many versions, and *Oedipus in Colonus* is a version of pastoral. Arcadia was always an atmosphere, though the actual Arcadia was itself, even in antiquity, a rugged and almost frightening terrain of untamed mountains.

The transforming of mere topographical space into scene —which might be termed the poetry of space—was achieved by a medieval artist like Dante, whose Purgatory and Paradise are elevations more atmospheric than cartographic. And Hell has its own sullen light. That other medieval poem, *The Romance of the Rose*, is, by contrast, topographical, a *hortus conclusus* like the settings in manuscript illuminations. But the twilight tonality of the Purgatorio and the blinding light of Paradise are psychic. The conversion of topographical setting into poetic scene often depends upon the play of light, which always modifies space.

An early Renaissance landscape like Konrad Witz's "Miraculous Draught of Fishes" is largely topographical, representing the shores of Lake Leman. Certain early Italian painters used Florence and its environs, notably the Val d'Arno, in much the same loco-descriptive way. Sometimes there was an infiltration of the fantastic. Benozzo Gozzoli's "Journey of the Magi" with its spiraling formulaic crags and stylized trees is an almost symbolic topography which, however, does not embrace its innumerable figures and episodes in an atmosphere. The miscellaneous narrative passages in this painting are presented in a fragmented perspective known as cavalier (a term probably derived from the half-medieval view of landscape as seen from a military platform giving a range of vision). This high point of view adapted itself to a serial development of a story unfolding in linear sequence, a composition that is illustrative and cartographic.

A major change in Renaissance painting came when this

cartographic vision was transvalued into ideal landscape by simplifying the composition and penetrating it with a quality of light never seen on land or sea, a light that fused the merely topographical features into a Virgilian harmony. We feel this new harmony in Giovanni Bellini's "Allegory of the Progress of the Soul," resonant with its coherent geometry, its pacific architecture, its sculptured promontories bathed in serene and unearthly light. We know how sensitive Leonardo was to light, how he treated his portraits and religious themes like the "Virgin and Child with St. Anne" in a tender gray register transfiguring the fantastic landscape into the atmosphere of the dream. The light intensifies in Tintoretto, and again in El Greco's vision of Toledo, which revises the old cavalier perspective into a nearly delirious illusion. Then Rembrandt and Vermeer, by the quality of their light, transvalued local and geometrically exact space into a tonality.

A harmonizing radiance had appeared in Fra Angelico, who has been said to rarefy sight into vision by his ethereal, half-medieval clarity. Speaking of Angelico, one critic has remarked that space is science without love and that light is science with love.[3] The harmony is devout in Angelico, but during the course of Renaissance painting it became secularized in the classic Arcadian vision, a legendary countergeography.

Yet Giorgione is the painter who most completely envelops his landscapes and figures in the alien distance of the dream. We still cannot identify the theme of the so-called "Tempest" (or "Stormy Landscape with Soldier and Gypsy"), but in spite of the seeming incoherence of the situation presented, nobody has failed to sense the harmony pervading the scene. The same deep, plangent harmony is heard in Titian, whether in his religious works like the "Deposition" or in the secular "Rape of Europa." The landscape with figures has a penumbral aspect in Tintoretto, whose phosphorescent light evaporates the flesh of

"Saint Mary of Egypt" and whose works sometimes have the acid vibrations of El Greco. By the 17th century this searching luminosity has so modified the geometry of painting—its spatial designations—that it has become a study in atmosphere as it has in Ruysdael's ghostly elegiac "Jewish Cemetery," one of the most solemn and affecting images landscape has ever offered, or Claude's mild radiance dissolving terrain and architecture and everything but the human figure into transparencies, or Poussin's symphonic vision of classic temples set so calmly in vistas open to the twilight of the gods.

This landscape tradition does not end with such painters but continues, in more demotic forms, into the 18th century with the so-called picturesque. Again it is notable that at this time there were two different sorts of landscape art: the loco-descriptive poem and painting (still topographical) and the picturesque. Most topographical poems and paintings were largely illustrative, limited to enumerating the features of a landscape. But from the early appearance of the picturesque in Milton's "L'Allegro" and "Il Penseroso," there is a feeling for the harmony or tonality pervading a geography. The picturesque did not belong to what Kenneth Clark calls "the landscape of fact" but to a rather sentimental vision that synthesizes topographical features into "keeping" (a term that meant a unifying tone). The 18th-century traveler used his "Claude glass" to harmonize the scene before him and to give it "keeping." Sometimes the picturesque is a revision of the old Arcadian vision of landscape, devalued, perhaps, into a middle-class mode as in Gainsborough's vernacular pastoral scenes or in Goldsmith's "Deserted Village," where sweet Auburn is Poussin without the classical apparatus. Yet even in this democratic guise the "keeping" regulates the tone or feeling.

The picturesque, in short, is a new version of the fantastic landscape, and it is an index of a psychic experience.

The tradition of landscape (or "scene"), whether it be Arcadian or merely picturesque, is able to recreate the world by its dreamlike quality. The world is not created anew in Canaletto's topographical paintings of Venice. But Guardi's vision of the same canals and piazzas is like a dream, for Guardi caught in his very touch and pigment the pulsation of Adriatic light that works a metamorphosis of actual places. Canaletto gives us a theatrical setting, scenographic. Guardi establishes a dramatic illusion, pictorial.

The relation between the poetic landscape and quietism is suggestive, especially when we contrast painting devoted to spatial analysis and painting devoted to light. To make a risky generality, one might say that the early Renaissance fascination with spatial organization—perspective—as we find it in Uccello, for instance, is marked by a restlessness and vigor of the mind associated with the new science, whereas painters who fused their vision by light spoke with a kind of quietism. One observes the contrast between Perugino's painfully geometric "Christ Giving the Keys to St. Peter" with its agitated figures in the background and its severe balance, and the reassuring calm of Giovanni Bellini's "Allegory of the Progress of the Soul," subordinating its geometry to a quality of illumination. In Leonardo there is a conflict between geometry and secretive tonality, and the tonality often gives a repose lacking in rigorously geometric structures. The light falling over and through ideal landscapes is a meditative substance suggesting arrest instead of change—the change that activates episodes depicted in foreshortened space.

So there is a difference between Renaissance ideal landscape and the later art of impressionism, which was also devoted to a quality of light. The light over the ideal (or fantastic) landscape was a constant; the light in impressionism is a transient effect. The half-scientific accuracy in early impressionism is a value different from the ideal light falling over Poussin's "Funeral of Phocion." Leonardo, to be sure, spoke of painting things seen in a twilight moment, but the blue distance of his backgrounds is hardly an impressionist vibration. Leonardo's blue light is a constant, a private but pondered benediction. Something of the same bemused constant is in the gray atmosphere of Giotto's frescoes, and it persists in Michelangelo's harmonies pervading the agitations of the "Last Judgment."

The changing light of impressionism traces back not to the ideal landscape or even to the fantastic landscape painted by Patinir but, instead, to the sensitivity of painters like Ruysdael and the Little Masters who watched clouds floating over Haarlem, modifying light by the hour. Yet through their study of momentary light the impressionists were gradually led back to constant harmonies of abstract color—a color that in Monet's abstractions was finally as meditative as the light dominating Giorgione's "Tempesta" or Poussin's classical fictions, subduing every feature to ideality.

There is a difference, too, between the Renaissance fantastic landscape and the impressionist landscape, for in the impressionist painting there is a uniform level of realization, whereas in the fantastic landscape of Patinir, Altdorfer, or Brueghel the planes of reality shift as they do in Shakespeare's plays. The fantastic landscape allowed interchanges of precision and imprecision, vague distances, vanishings into worlds not realized but only suggested. These shifting planes of reality appear as early as Jan Van Eyck's "Madonna of Chancellor Rolin": in the foreground the figures, quite hieratic, of Virgin, Child, and donor, then immediately behind, in almost grotesque perspective, the tiny figures standing on a balcony, looking backwards out of the picture toward the fantastic landscape with its curved bridge and, further still, in a poetic distance, dreamlike islets, castles, promontories, ships, and far snowy mountains, blue and airy. Realism against the visionary. The same shifting planes of representation are in Grüne-

wald, in Lucas van Leyden, in Altdorfer. They are essential
to the poetry of the fantastic landscape which, like Donne's
poetry, could assimilate every plane of experience in an
"imperative dream."

Such interchanges in space imply interchanges in time:
the present moment in the foreground, the timeless in the
background—the local against the universal. So to speak,
the foreground is in punctual time and the background is
in psychic time, the time of the dream or "vision."
Throughout our discussion of Shakespearean drama we
have, in general, found these two sorts of time. The chronometric time is episodic, isolating acts in sequence; the
psychic time is an experience of interpenetrating moments
in a continuum that expresses a quality of selfhood, a condition that is like a fourth dimension in human life. This
fourth dimension has a moral meaning, as where Othello
says, unconscious of his reference, that when he does not
love Desdemona chaos is come *again*. Chaos was always
there, and the dramatic events are simply the occasions for
disclosing this inherent chaos.

In some Shakespearean plays psychic time is a reflex of
the psychic landscape we have been calling fantastic or
poetic with its shifting planes of reality, its "charmed"
atmosphere. The deeper unity in such plays is expressed in
the quality of scene or, in a metaphorical sense, the landscape in which the action takes place. Notably in the later
plays the drama is scenic insofar as the entire action is
absorbed into, or pervaded by, an atmosphere, which G.
Wilson Knight calls its symbolic or poetic space. In these
plays the setting is not a mere topographical circumstance
but becomes a fourth or psychic dimension scenically as
well as chronologically. So also in Renaissance painting can
we imagine Giorgione's "Sleeping Venus" in another landscape? This fourth dimension is the larger *opsis*.

Georges Poulet has said that spatial representation requires a certain exclusiveness of point of view. This is

especially true of vanishing point perspective, which restricted space much as a chronometric view or sequence restricted time. Yet there is another way of experiencing space, just as there is another way of experiencing time. Space can be atmospheric just as time can be durative. And when space is atmospheric it is not schematic, just as when time is durative it is not sequential. As G. Wilson Knight remarks, although the time sequence may be present to consciousness, the poetic atmosphere in Shakespeare tends "to be unconsciously apprehended or created, a half-realized significance, a vague all-inclusive deity of the dramatic universe." This atmospheric space penetrates and qualifies "the plot-chain of event following event" like "the omnipresent and mysterious reality brooding motionless over and within the play's movement."

Vanishing point perspective is schematic just as the mechanics of plot are schematic. But Shakespeare's theatre, with its unschematic space and multiple points of view, was not so restrictive as the proscenium stage. The Elizabethan stage has been compared to the open beam structure we see in paintings like Botticelli's "Adoration of the Magi," where the birth of Christ takes place under a scaffolding beyond and above which extend landscape and sky, a representation of space that is at once local and cosmic. This open stage fostered atmospheric effects available to painters of fantastic landscapes, where towns, seas, mountains synthesize every kind of local episode into a poetic vision. Frances Yates has called this the *idea* of a theatre which is cosmic, as Vitruvian architecture was cosmic. Such poetic space is a vehicle of freedom.

In this large sense many Shakespearean plays are created within the tradition of fantastic landscape, making their enveloping atmosphere a quality of experience. Indeed it might be said that there are two sorts of Shakespearean play: where space is used schematically, and where space is used poetically as a fourth or psychic dimension. That is, some plays have a mere local setting (as in *Julius Caesar*) and some have a poetic atmosphere *(The Tempest)*. Generally speaking, the plays of local setting are schematic not only in space but in time, chronology being of primary importance. These are plays of closure, just as the rigorously orthogonal paintings of the Italian Renaissance are closures.

In *Comedy of Errors*, for example, there is no landscape but only setting, which happens to be Ephesus, standing in contrast to Syracuse simply by legality. It is a play notably lacking psychological or poetic envelopment. The reworking of this mechanical plot in *Twelfth Night* affords a kind of atmosphere, for Illyria with its music has the rudiments of a poetic dimension absent in the earlier play. The equations of mistaken identity remain, but the whole action is keyed to a double tonality that could be disturbing were it more fully realized. The context of the main action is melodious, as suggested by Orsino's opening sentimental speech:

> If music be the food of love, play on,
> Give me excess of it, that surfeiting
> The appetite may sicken, and so die.

Yet in the background there is another sinister tonality of persecution, mockery, and even social conflict in the humbling of Malvolio, and Olivia's last remark ("Alas, poor fool, how have they baffled thee!") is filled with an easy contempt grounded in a security of genteel privilege that can safely rebuke a bounder. When Malvolio exits with his threatening line, "I'll be revenged on the whole pack of you," we can already hear the sullen revolt that did not become fully audible until the revolutionary mania of 1789. But it would be hard to claim that *Twelfth Night*, in spite of its sentimental obbligato, is much less schematic than *Comedy of Errors*. Illyria is still a setting, not a scene.

Romeo and Juliet is a kindred case. Shakespeare seldom

wrote a play more local in setting or more schematic in chronology. "There is no world without Verona walls," exclaims Romeo, and the two and forty hours of Juliet's misadventured sleep, along with the changed date of the wedding to Paris, and the mistimed appearance of Romeo at the tomb are chronometric devices that betray the artifice of plot. The mechanical opposition of Montagu and Capulet is like the mechanical composition that balances figure against figure in the schematic painting of the Renaissance. In fact, the play depends upon contrived manipulations in scale, Romeo seeming heroic against Paris, Mercutio looking humane against the vicious Tybalt, Juliet looking innocent against the worldly nurse and natural against the tinsel image of Rosaline, Romeo's devotion to Juliet appearing authentic against his first courtly posturing. In this star-crossed action fate is chronometric misfortune. The only atmospheric effect arises from the pervading contrast of hot and glaring noon with the splendor of love-performing night, which is associated with the macabre beauty of the tomb, where Juliet's maids are worms and where Death sets up his pale ensign. There is no transcendence of time and the hour, for there is finality when Romeo says, "Thus with a kiss I die." The intensity of passion is largely an intensity of rhetoric. Neither time nor space is here a vehicle of freedom, and the composition must be seen from a fixed point of view; the world of *Romeo and Juliet* is unified, but at some cost.

By contrast *The Merchant of Venice* is a play of divided worlds that are never harmonized but held in a ruptured or double perspective: the sordid world of the Rialto and the romantic world of Belmont. In this strange dramatic coexistence there is implied a fissured view of life and humanity, a duplicity all the more remarkable in that the world of Belmont is an early venture in creating a poetic atmosphere—a venture that fails, unlike the later ventures in *Cymbeline, Winter's Tale,* or *The Tempest.* The world of the Rialto is in clear local focus, whereas the potentially romantic world of Belmont, a world of music, moonlight, and happily gained fortune, is a kind of fantastic landscape that never quite establishes itself convincingly. Behind these two worlds are unreconciled points of view, or, more accurately, two points of view that should be different, and are not. For the Rialto and Belmont are both worlds of bonding.

Supposedly the Rialto is the locus where bonds are enforced, and supposedly Belmont is the locus where bonds are loosened by love, romance, and free expenditure. Yet in Belmont there are the prescriptions of a father's will, the bonding of Portia's lovers, the bonding of exchanged rings, the final bonding of Shylock's fortune. Significantly enough, the only locus where the two worlds intersect is in court, where the precisions of law are enforced by the exactions of Shylock, then the exactions of the letter of the law by Portia. And in both worlds the law can be juggled. The atmosphere of Belmont is not fully liberating, for Belmont is the Rialto translated to another plane. The two worlds are different and the two worlds are the same, with the same values of gold in each, gold being gained on the Rialto by one means, gold being gained in Belmont by another. The psychology of the Rialto is purportedly different from the psychology of Belmont, but they are akin.

Music in Belmont does not work its spell as it does in Giorgione's "Fête Champêtre," for Belmont is not, after all, an Arcadian world. It is simply a domain where acquisition occurs by stratagems less direct than those on the Rialto. Belmont lacks the authentic blue distance. The exclusive point of view that makes Shylock alien on the Rialto also makes Morocco alien in Belmont: "Let all of his complexion choose me so," says Portia disdainfully. And Bassanio, the wastrel and fortune-hunter, is the only intermediary between two spheres of experience that should be dissimilar and are too similar. The planes of reality do not really shift.

To use a phrase from art criticism, *The Merchant of Venice*

presents two topographies, Venice and Belmont. Landscape in Giorgione's "Sleeping Venus" and "The Tempest" is more than topography, it is a new and transcendent
poetry. The landscape in Poussin's "Funeral of Phocion"
or Claude's "Acis and Galatea" is not topography but another register of experience—a learned dream, to be sure,
but one establishing a pictorial environment where every
feature is harmonized into full concord. The ordinary
world has dropped away, and there appears what Baudelaire called a composition for which nature is only a dictionary. Baudelaire remarks that imaginative painters seek in
this dictionary of nature "for the elements which suit their
conception; in adjusting those elements, however, with
more or less of art, they confer upon them a totally new
physiognomy." Thus "a good picture, which is the faithful
equivalent of the dream which has begotten it, should be
brought into being like a world."[4] The world created anew
in the Renaissance landscape-with-figures is not a rear-
rangement of topography but the establishment of another
order, a reality wrought, as Coleridge said, only by a poetic
power that "dissolves, diffuses, dissipates, in order to recreate."

Another Shakespearean play that is topographical instead of imaginative in this sense is *As You Like It,* where
again we find two juxtaposed worlds, Duke Frederick's
court and the Forest of Arden, a world apart but not a
recreated world. Amiens's song about lying under the
greenwood tree provides a setting but hardly an atmosphere, and there is something merely theatrical about the
whole situation in which disguise is so important. In the
landscape-with-figures, the figures are not only transposed
from one setting to another, they belong to another order
of being, like the soldier (if he is a soldier) and the woman
in Giorgione's "Tempest." Rosalind and Celia are figures
exiled from court, but their natures do not change in
Arden. Their very disguise lends meaning to Jaques's rhet-

oric about all the world being a stage and men and women players. The calm and classic figures in Poussin's "Et In Arcadia Ego" are not players in this sense but beings more radically transfigured, begotten of their new world. The painting is drama, not theatre, a drama in which the personages do not simply play roles but represent a heightened coefficient of experience. The Forest of Arden is a strange world, but essentially a theatrical construct, fanciful but hardly dreamlike. The poetry of space is not fully achieved.

In that remarkable early play, *Love's Labour's Lost*, there is abrupt change from one sort of spatial effect to another, from setting to environment or atmosphere. The action begins in a setting as contrived and artificial as anything in Renaissance theatre, the institution of an academy governed by an asceticism of the mind. This regime of false humanism is a closure of experience, and the topography of the early scenes is amusingly local. One of the finer effects in this play is the theatrical posturing, a role-playing that inspires not only disguisings but a satire upon life lived in art form. For four and three-quarter acts the play proceeds in its foreshortened manner. Then suddenly while the company watches the absurd spectacle of the Nine Worthies comes the news of the King of France's death. Berowne is the first to sense that the acting is over, exclaiming "Worthies away! The scene begins to cloud." At once the entire milieu changes. No Shakespearean play more abruptly breaks out of its theatrical confines. The closing passages are not only inconclusive, their tone is sober and half-penitential, for an entirely different world is immediately suggested by the King's death.

The change in tone is prepared by the mockery of the Nine Worthies playlet, which reduces to absurdity the role-playing of the lords. This must be abandoned for another kind of role-playing that returns experience from art form to life. It is almost as if Shakespeare were commenting upon the failure of art to cope with human experience.

Another kind of acting will be required if the lords are to win their ladies. There is a shift from the artifice of the academic setting to an enveloping atmosphere that is tantalizing in its ambiguity and shadowed with an intuition of grief and, at its extreme, suffering. The Dark Lady Rosaline, who is hardly eligible to respond to the grimness of sickness and death, imposes upon Berowne an act demanding humility: to make the moribund laugh. Berowne is shocked; he doubts that he can bring laughter in the throat of death. Yet Rosaline assures him that this is the way to choke his gibing spirit. So the play ends with the strange and rasping adieu by Armado, "The words of Mercury are harsh after the songs of Apollo. You that way; we this way." This change in temper is associated, as Philip Edwards notes, with a change in the time scheme of the play. Up to the moment of death the pace is episodic, then there comes a retard, a pause, with an implication of future experience in slow, monotonous durative time.

The unexpected shadowed ending of the play is hardly elegiac, and yet there is an echo of Poussin's "Et In Arcadia Ego" with its timeless calm. This classic world of meditative resignation has been described by Erwin Panofsky: "Poussin's Louvre picture no longer shows a dramatic encounter with Death but a contemplative absorption in the idea of mortality. We are confronted with a change from thinly veiled moralism to undisguised elegiac sentiment."[5] The final passages of *Love's Labour's Lost* absorb the feeling that man is not entirely master of his fate, and a recognition that "purifies itself and turns to grace." The darkening of the scene transforms the early fashionable nonsense into a closing intimation of human failure, pain, and helplessness. Unlike *The Merchant of Venice*, *Love's Labour's Lost* does actually offer two different worlds as alternatives. However briefly, an atmosphere is established as it is not in Belmont. Though the change from the world of the Academe to the world of the sick and dying is only projected, Berowne enters a new environment.

Characteristically, Shakespeare's most dramatic feats are performed in unwonted places. A play as light-hearted as *Midsummer Night's Dream* is perhaps the first in which there appears a poetic world created by scene. Here again is a play with two worlds, Athens and the fairy realm; or shall we say three worlds, for there is the dramatic world of the interlude; or possibly four worlds if we include the world of the rehearsal, where a dramatic illusion is being evolved. These worlds are fused by the wonder of everyone. The world of Athens is no less fantastic landscape than the world of the fairy king and queen. The visionary texture of the entire play is suggested by Hermia's recollection of her moonlight aberration:

> Methinks I see these things with parted eye,
> When everything seems double. (IV, 1)

One thinks of Blake's double vision. Demetrius, looking back on the night, has the double vision of a painter like Brueghel, finding that it seems like far-off mountains turned to clouds; and Hippolyta judges that however fanciful these images are, they have great constancy "strange and admirable." Even Bottom is translated by his dream, a "rare vision" he cannot expound. Theseus has his own faculty of wonder, for he can look on the wretched performance of the interlude, seeing it in all its absurdity, yet comprehending that "the best in this kind are but shadows." Theseus's sanity is an ability to transform actuality to illusion by his generous vision, taking the will for the deed.

Midsummer Night's Dream is so penetrated by illusion that all its worlds are atmospheric. What might pass for the world of actuality—Athens—is itself as legendary as the Arcadian world posited by Poussin or Giorgione. The irony is that, by an unexpected reversal, the only "real" world is the theatrical world of the interlude contrived by the mechanicals when they try to enact Pyramus and Thisby. In their literal-mindedness they intend to depend

upon actual moonlight for lunar radiance, and must explain, in their anxiety to reassure their audience, that the
theatrical lion is but a man costumed as a beast. The most
actual world is the world that is a basis for drama as the
pedestrian mentality conceives it. The rustic mind is
caught in the toils of fact, unable to validate the dramatic
illusion with which Theseus endows their show. This implication that the dramatic world is a false world is a baffl-
ing return of Shakespeare upon the fabrications of his own
art. In short, the world of the interlude as presented by the
mechanicals is the only world that is not transformed.

The "real" world of Athens, in contrast to the fairy
world of night, is already another realm of experience as
credible and incredible as the fancied world of Tasso's
Jerusalem Delivered, Sidney's *Arcadia,* or Spenser's *Faerie
Queene.* It establishes its own atmosphere in which Hermia
must wed Demetrius upon pain of Athenian penalty of
dying the death or being mewed in cloister to chant faint
hymns to the cold moon. This, by another reversal or
irony, is precisely the world of those antique fables Theseus scorns as being born of the poet's seething brain, giving to airy nothing a local habitation and name. Yet Athens
maintains itself as firmly in the imagination as Poussin's
Arcadian landscapes. It is a world founded upon some credence inaccessible to the modern mind. Upon such credence much Renaissance culture was built. The world of
Athens is one of the fiduciary structures Renaissance art
achieved. It enabled Pieter Brueghel to paint "The Fall of
Icarus," with an ordinary plowman doing his daily tasks in
the foreground and in the background the classical, visionary, legendary world that haunted, abidingly, the arts of
the Renaissance. The quotidian could be placed, like Bottom and the mechanicals, in a fantastic perspective, a
fiduciary structure we have lost. To the Elizabethan mind
"Athens" was not historical but a timeless, liberating vision. In what sense did Shakespeare's audience "believe"
this fiduciary structure?

How completely these fiduciary structures are alien to our modern imagination is indicated by Oberon's behest to Puck to fetch the little flower whose deluding juice is to be squeezed upon lovers' eyes. How, we ask, did the Elizabethans believe—or disbelieve—the references in Oberon's speech, which suggests the "multi-consciousness" of the Renaissance mind, its access to worlds from which we have been exiled, for Oberon is referring to magic, to the science which was partly magic, to the strangely fancied geography of new worlds, to Queen Elizabeth and her politics of virginity, to classic legend, to contemporary medicine and physiology—to we know not how much else. It is an astonishing compendium, especially since it is in the mouth of a fairy king:

> That very time I saw (but thou couldst not)
> Flying between the cold moon and the earth
> Cupid all armed. A certain aim he took
> At a fair vestal, throned by the west,
> And loosed his love-shaft smartly from his bow,
> As it should pierce a hundred thousand hearts.
> But I might see young Cupid's fiery shaft
> Quenched in the chaste beams of the wat'ry moon,
> And the imperial vot'ress passed on,
> In maiden meditation, fancy-free.
> Yet marked I where the bolt of Cupid fell.
> It fell upon a little western flower,
> Before milk-white, now purple with love's wound.
> And maidens call it love-in-idleness.
> Fetch me that flower: the herb I showed thee once.
> The juice of it on sleeping eyelids laid,
> Will make or man or woman madly dote
> Upon the next live creature that it sees.
> Fetch me this herb, and be thou here again
> Ere the Leviathan can swim a league. (II, 1)

How *did* the Elizabethans believe in Cupid, and what credence did they give to the effects of pansy juice? In this speech we have the key to the means by which the Renaissance mind established landscapes we call fantastic. Whatever it was, this credence made the Renaissance vision possible. The Renaissance had the great advantage referred to by Wallace Stevens when he urges belief in a fiction that we know to be a fiction: "The exquisite truth is to know that it is a fiction and that you believe in it willingly." There being nothing else, adds Stevens. Shakespeare would understand. And the good will by which Theseus, the realist, picks a welcome from the stumbling Latin of the clerk who greets him is also a fiduciary act that might be called charity. So too when Theseus looks at the interlude and imagines as well of Bottom and his fellows as they imagine of themselves, he converts the shortcomings of mere theatre into a charitable vision that becomes drama.

This fiduciary imagination transforms the landscape of fact to Arcadia or to the world of Theseus and Oberon. It is the premise of poetic drama. Shakespeare says as much in the prologues to *Henry V*, which call attention to the dozen vile and ragged foils which the audience must take to be armies at Agincourt, "minding true things by what their mockeries be." In these prologues Shakespeare is *in propria persona* repeating what the journeyman spoke as prologue to Pyramus and Thisby. As fiduciary structure, drama must be poetic much as the ideal landscape of Renaissance painting is poetic. The fidiciary structures of the middle ages were religious; the fiduciary structures of the Renaissance were secular and cultural fictions visible in the landscape-with-figures and in plays like *Midsummer Night's Dream*. At the close Puck speaks almost like Baudelaire in saying that these visions have the yielding of a dream.

Today we distinguish between the primary and the secondary dream elaboration, for the dream "told over" when we awake is not the dream we dreamed. The primary nocturnal dream has the authentic psychic landscape, enveloping, insistent as a dominant chord. In the secondary retelling this psychic tonality is likely to escape. Sometimes the

Renaissance landscape retains the psychic atmosphere of the primary dream, as it does in Leonardo's blue distances or the nearly psychedelic effects in Elsheimer, Patinir, or Altdorfer, and in Tintoretto also. Sometimes it is closer to the secondary dream elaboration—closer to surrealism—when it is not fully submerged in the psychic atmosphere but merely illustrative. For example, the episodes in Piero di Cosimo's paintings are outlandish, but the psychic temper is thinned, and Piero, like many surrealists, seems to be a quaint illustrator instead of a truly visionary painter. For one thing, in seeing a Piero we are tempted to ask exactly *what* incident is taking place. But in Giorgone's "Tempest" the incident does not so much matter as the tonal saturation, which absorbs the incident. In the primary dream the episodes are immersed in an ambience that is like a pictorial constant, making the environment more expressive than the episodes. With its perfectly articulated episodes *Midsummer Night's Dream* resembles the secondary dream elaboration.

Macbeth has a more sinister psychic charge and is closer to the mysterious region of the primary dream. We have already mentioned the anachronisms in this play, its condensation, the present, the past, and the future coexisting in the timeless guilty consciousness of Macbeth. It is a truly nocturnal play with the affliction of dreams shaking the single state of man. The primary world of this drama is the subliminal darkness where Macbeth lives. The atmosphere is seeling night, scarfing up pitiful day; the light thickens until the heavens are obscured. As has been said, the porter scene is central, for Dunsinane is an inferno where Macbeth is isolated. It has been conjectured that Middleton, not Shakespeare, wrote the scenes with the witches, but even if so, these scenes belong to the psychic landscape enveloping the play. Here is a kind of counterpoint to the holy precincts in *Oedipus in Colonus,* where we hear other and milder chthonic voices. The witches are voices of an-

other underworld—the underworld of the abyssal Id. Such
voices are also oracular, audible in dreams. Macbeth's life
becomes a waking dream, a kind of living nightmare. His
present fears are less real to him than his horrible imaginings, and his fantastical future murdering is so vivid to him
that "function/ Is smothered in surmise, and nothing is/
But what is not."

In *Macbeth* the dream is *lived* as it is not in *Midsummer
Night's Dream,* and thus the ambiguity is deeper, the relation between the two worlds more problematic and disturbed. The world of Athens and the fairy world are fantastic landscapes; the landscape in *Macbeth* is more radically
poetic. Lady Macbeth lives in actuality except at night, but
her husband lives continually in the nightmare landscape
where green seas are incarnadined. This psychic landscape
belongs to another category than space. To be sure, *Macbeth*
has its own spatial design, for as in *Othello* the play begins
from the outside, from afar, and draws inward vortically
toward nocturnal Dunsinane. So too *Othello* moves inevitably from the Moor's distant campaigns to Venice, to Cyprus, and lastly to the deathly chamber. And this spatial
centripetalism is echoed in the vortical acceleration of time.
Always in *Macbeth* this spatial movement occurs in a psychic climate, the psychography that is like a menace.

The psychography is otherwise in *Lear,* a play as centrif-
ugal as *Macbeth* is centripetal. The annihilating explosion
of the Lear world is symbolized by the repeated "out, out,"
"away, away," and the unnatural fracturing of every
familial bond. Spatially, *Lear* begins at a focal point, the
court of the aged king, and expands quickly in all directions
toward the chaos of a world gone to pieces, into outer
darkness. The atmosphere in *Lear* is the ultimate anti-
Arcadian vision, cracking Nature's molds. This psychic
landscape makes the paintings by Hieronymus Bosch look
benign. In a world where one's daughters are a disease in
one's flesh or a corruption in the blood, where one's flesh
is so vile that it begets only hate, the topology is as savage

as in some of the deluges drawn by Leonardo, whose visionary disasters are actually endured by Lear. The tempest in *Lear* is no mere setting; it is the collapse of the mind and the demolition of a vision of man as a creature noble in reason, infinite in faculties, angelic in apprehension. *Lear* is the *Götterdämmerung* of Renaissance humanism, and Shakespeare furnishes the required scene.

One of the miracles of the last plays is the revision of the unendurable Lear environment and the creation of scenes in which man is redeemed. In these plays there remain the anguish of injustice, the vileness of treachery, the folly of lust, the stench of the bawdy house, and the criminal instincts of ambitious or suspicious minds—but all in a new context, in a psychography that magically brings remission of sin. This strange access to peace that passes understanding can hardly be only the result of writing for an indoor theatre. Possibly it generates in a vision of man in a new landscape as fantastic as the seacoast of Bohemia. For the distancing in the later plays is consistent: not idyllic, though there are idyllic episodes, and certainly not always Arcadian, though prevailingly open to "another" world. In these plays the resolution occurs in a transforming atmosphere that somehow suspends the moral consequences of sordid events preceding a mutation by scene.

This new distancing is often temporal as well as scenic, as the prologue to the fourth act of *Winter's Tale* suggests, for time can put the wrongs of the past in a solacing perspective, healing and elegiac. At such distances man recovers a lost innocence and regains a faculty for tolerance and forgiveness that has been injured or even destroyed by antecedent experience. Often there is no assignable motive for these sudden reversals in temperament; they simply come—as if without conscious volition—when the character finds himself in another scene or when Time "in one self-born hour" tries all, "both joy and terror/ Of good and bad, that makes and unfolds error."

Among the plays of redemption is *Pericles*, which is sul-

lied by the degradation of the bawdy house where Boult
has the repulsive task of deflowering Marina, a situation
more sordid than anything in *Measure for Measure*. "Faith,
I must ravish her, or she'll disfurnish us of all our caval-
leria." The resolution in *Measure for Measure* and *All's Well
That Ends Well* does not depend upon scene, but *Pericles* is
different, as T. S. Eliot saw, for Marina is a creature who
comes from another world, the seascape that was spiritu-
ally her parentage:

> Thou that wast born at sea, buried at Tharsus,
> And found at sea again. (V, 1)

The sea change of Prospero's isle is already working its
effect.

Pericles is as ugly as *Cymbeline*, which is built upon characters like the viciously tyrannical king and his no less
vicious queen, and Clóten, a reeking monster resembling
Caliban. In a ghastly parody of Othello's mistrust, Posthumus, with a depraved sporting impulse, makes his vile
wager that the yellow Iachimo cannot seduce Imogen, stak-
ing gold for gold. The Moor could not have entered upon
such an obscene venture. Imogen's bedchamber, a scene of
Titian-like *luxe, calme, et volupté*, has the theatricality of the
masque, but the treachery and hatred of the play are not
modified until the action moves afield into the idyllic landscape of Wales, the cave where Belarius lives with Cymbeline's sons. This landscape is tempered by the music of
the elegy for golden lads and girls who come to dust. At the
masque-like close, Posthumus dreams of Jupiter descending in thunder from another world, a *deus ex machina* to
reconcile discords:

> No more, you petty spirits of regions low,
> Offend our hearing. Hush! . . .
> Poor shadows of Elysium, hence, and rest
> Upon your never-withering banks of flowers.
> Be not with mortal accidents oppressed. (V, 4)

The changed atmosphere works its magic on the yellow Iachimo sinking to repentance, and on Posthumus, who already has washed away his hate:

> For Imogen's dear life take mine . . .
> 'Tween man and man they weigh not every stamp;
> Though light, take pieces for the figure's sake.
>   . . . And so, great powers,
> If you will take this audit, take this life
> And cancel these cold bonds. (V, 4)

The quality of mercy, so strained in *The Merchant of Venice*, where bonds stay uncancelled even in Belmont, changes everything in these final scenes. The artificial landscape of Renaissance vision had ethical overtones.

Reconciliation by scene is similar in *The Winter's Tale*, another action that begins in hatred and mistrust. For Leontes, like Posthumus, is as cruelly jealous as Othello, and with less reason, since there is no poisonous Iago to stir suspicion. Without any motive whatever Leontes has drunk and "seen the spider":

> Is whispering nothing?
> Is leaning cheek to cheek? Is meeting noses?
> Kissing with inside lip? stopping the career
> Of laughter with a sigh?—a note infallible
> Of breaking honesty! (I, 2)

The infection in Leontes's mind taints the Sicilian climate. But there is another climate on the seacoast of Bohemia where Perdita, like Marina, is saved and, under the pastoral tutelage of the old shepherd and Autolycus, becomes an agent for reconciliation. In *Winter's Tale* and *Cymbeline* there are two worlds, the court and the idyl, and the temper of the idyllic world purifies the atmosphere at court.

In both cases, also, the distancing in idyllic space is a distancing in time. The Arcadian world was a nostalgic vision, and Erwin Panofsky has defined the difference between the Renaissance and medieval time senses, between the proto-Renaissance of the 12th century and the later Italian Renaissance. Both periods were familiar with antiquity and freely employed classical iconography. But the tendency in medieval arts was to update the past, presenting classical figures and legends as contemporary and obliterating the time dimension not through ignorance of the past but through a failure to imagine the existence of another antique world. So there are two Renaissances, and the second established its dream of an Arcadian order. The ability to dream into being another world distanced in time gave the Arcadian landscape its elegiac tone—we were once, too, in Arcadia. Panofsky remarks:

> Arcady emerged from the past like an enchanting vision. Only, for the modern mind, this Arcady was not so much a Utopia of bliss and beauty distant in space as a Utopia of bliss and beauty distant in time. Like the whole classical sphere, of which it had become an integral part, Arcady became an object of that nostalgia which distinguishes the real Renaissance from all those pseudo or proto-Renaissances that had taken place during the Middle Ages: it developed into a haven, not only from a faulty reality, but also, and even more so, from a questionable present. . . . Soon . . . the visionary kingdom of Arcady was re-established as a sovereign domain. ("Poussin and the Elegiac Tradition")

Valéry once said that man is a creature who feels the need for what does not exist, and he adds that any true culture requires the presence of absent things. The Arcadian vision gives a new resource to Renaissance culture.

The visionary final world of *Antony and Cleopatra* is not elegiac or Arcadian; it is Elysian, and Elysium was one of the remoter domains in the classical tradition. No Shakespearean play more potently establishes its imaginary worlds, three of them—the world of Roman politics governed by Caesar, the world of Nilotic Egypt given to an erotic humanism of the flesh, and the Elysian world open to Antony and Cleopatra after they have put behind them the other two worlds. This play confirms the hegemony of the Renaissance imagination, which distanced in time as well as in space. Magnificently scenic as it is, the action ranges over the Caesarian empire from Rome to Parthia, each province having its own atmosphere. The Roman world is of rigorous honor, decency, and obligation, a half-puritan world of duty recognized and accepted. In the alien world of Egypt every woman's palm presages fertility, and Cleopatra, wrinkled deep in time, is black with amorous pinches. The visionary world which Antony begins to discern when Rome and Egypt fall away is born of black vesper's pageants:

> Sometime we see a cloud that's dragonish,
> A vapor sometime like a bear or lion,
> A towered citadel, a pendant rock,
> A forked mountain, or blue promontory
> With trees upon it, that nod unto the world
> And mock our eyes with air. (IV, 14)

Antony is glimpsing the horizons that are foyers to another world. He believes he can enter this vista to overtake Cleopatra:

> . . . I come, my queen . . .
> Where souls do couch on flowers, we'll hand in hand,
> And with our sprightly port make the ghosts gaze:
> Dido and her Aeneas shall want troops,
> And all the haunt be ours. (IV, 14)

Cleopatra falls under the spell of this vision for which she has prepared herself by sailing on her burnished throne down the Nile in a pageant beggaring description and "o'erpicturing that Venus where we see/ The fancy outwork nature." (Titian had already had the vision in his "Recumbent Venus.") So she performs her noble Roman act, embarking for that other eternal Cydnus where she will greet Antony in a realm that transcends Roman and Egyptian space and time. It is said that Cleopatra's last illusion is her first reality. The envisioned Elysium transfigures the very nature of the queen ("Husband, I come."), her evasive death enabling her to escape Caesar and to fulfill the possibilities of her dramatic imagination.

Hamlet had an intensely dramatic imagination but never found the arena in which it could be expressed; his dramatic representations do not catch the conscience of the king or resolve the conflicts within himself. He could not create the drama he needed. Cleopatra has this privilege at the moment of her death, making her fire and air. This transfiguring could not have occurred without the imperial Egyptian scene she is able to command. Nor could Titian have transfigured his Venus without the scene in which she so calmly and majestically lies, her flesh becoming the triumphant illusion of another world. For Hamlet time was neurosis, and in *Othello* and *Lear* and *Troilus and Cressida* time is injurious in a variety of ways, through haste or senility or disillusion. All these injuries are healed in the Elysian perspective that projects Cleopatra out of history, out of the casualties of Fortune that destroyed Romeo and Juliet. Only after the abundance of the Nilotic scene could Antony and Cleopatra have found their new haven.

The farthest reach of pictorial imagination is the sea change in Prospero's kingdom. It is a kingdom that does not exclude the murderous Antonio, who would quiet Alonso with three inches of steel. But it is a kingdom where evil is negated by music and the magic that is an instrument of fate. In the backward of time there was a change Antonio worked by new-creating Prospero's subjects in Milan to an evil nature; then there is the change in Prospero's isle where twangling sounds make even Caliban dream of a cloudy world until he cries to dream again. In this alien world man finds his own nature, being most himself when he is least his own, all things changed from what they were in Milan and Naples. Under this spell Antonio is silenced, negated, and the evil in the others washed away:

> And as the morning steals upon the night,
> Melting the darkness, so their rising senses
> Begin to chase the ignorant fumes that mantle
> Their clearer reason. (V, 1)

Under such charm Caliban learns to be wise and seek for grace. It is a transfiguration that takes us back to the grove in Colonus, that precinct where the afflicted Oedipus also found that time is a version of mercy and that man is eligible for some mysterious levitation that seems almost sacrosanct. Prospero, finding that the rarer act is in forgiveness than in vengeance, gains this wisdom and reaches this reconciliation by a perspective opening like Leonardo's blue distance into a vision that is the supreme fabric of Renaissance art, a landscape that is the stuff of dreams.

The Tempest is a scenic determination of life. Ariel hovers above Antonio and Sebastian with their drawn swords and thwarts their Macbeth-like crime with the warning, "You fools: I and my fellows/ Are ministers of fate." The visionary world of Prospero has the valency of the tragic world with its extremes of innocence and evil. As Gonzalo says, "All torment, trouble, wonder, and amazement/ Inhabits here." The planes of reality shift until the idyl is implicit in tragedy, music in tempest, and moral laws seem to operate by some poetic code.

In this play, as in Rembrandt, we can study what happened in Renaissance art, which at first organized the substance of the world into a topography—a coherent and systematic space—by thinking a structure into being; then the substance dissolves, as it does in Rembrandt's etchings, where the material shimmers off into modulations of light, and all that is dense to hand or eye is illumined from within or is enveloped by an aurora beating upon it from without.

There is a transubstantiation, a metamorphosis from plastic to visionary, a mutation from the actual into the luminous. Christ, hanging in agony on the cross, is absorbed into a burst of light that showers down quiveringly from some primal radiance bestowed upon the crucifiers and the crucified, submerging the evil, the pain, the cruelty in a somber hallowed twilight, a pure tonality. Rembrandt never denied the bitterness of Calvary, but transvalued it to a fabric of vision, just as Prospero transvalues the wickedness and torment on his isle into the stuff of dreams. Like Rembrandt, Prospero presses the scenic resolution to a final harmony begotten of his world.

Dante too is visionary, but anatomized the world by degrees and limits, planes of reality that do not shift. The *Commedia* can be read four ways: literally, anagogically, morally, and allegorically. We do not know how to read *The Tempest* by such designated categories of meaning; we can only read it poetically.

The conquest of evil was difficult for Prospero; this has rightly been called a severe play. Like Plato, Prospero combats our lawless wild beast nature. Possibly the last evil for Prospero abides in cynicism, the Antonio malady. Antonio is, like Iago, an anti-poetic mind who sees the world in parts instead of by total vision. Antonio is committed to tactics without having the distanced view of life as a fabric of vision. Caliban the beastlike can be enlightened and seek grace, but the silent and cynical Antonio can resist the human spirit confident in its forgiving, its insight into sin, a tolerance and insight that secure a triumph, a recognition that competes with the tragic recognition. This triumph is not won except against the flesh and the will, and then perhaps only for a moment in a scene created by a wholly poetic consciousness.

Notes

I. *The Measures of Time: Four Time Schemes*

1. Mabel Buland in *The Presentation of Time in Elizabethan Drama* analyzes the use of double or stretched time in Shakespeare.

2. Clifford Leech, "The Structure of the Last Plays," *Shakespeare Survey*, No. 11.

3. Theodore Weiss in *The Breath of Clowns and Kings* (1971) argues that the strawberry incident is entirely in character and a useful dramatic shift.

4. In speaking of the *Eigenwelt*, I adapt the comment of Ludwig Binswanger (*Ausgewaelte Vortraege und Aufsaetze*, Bern, 1947) as mentioned by Rollo May in: "The Existential Approach," *American Handbook of Psychiatry II* (1959): 1355. Binswanger considers the *Eigenwelt* to be "not merely subjective inner experience" but a sense of our own orientation to reality.

II. *Political Time: The Vanity of History*

1. The following "scale reduction" of history is drawn from Hans Kalmus, "Organic Evolution and Time," in: J. T. Fraser, *The Voices of Time*, p. 332. Kalmus is quoting B. Hocking.

III. *Lived Time and Thought Time: The Privileged Moment*

1. The point is made by Paul Fraisse in *The Psychology of Time*, trans. J. Leith.

2. Jean Piaget, "Time Perception in Children," in: Fraser, *The Voices of Time*, p. 202ff.

3. Robbe-Grillet, *La Maison de Rendez-Vous*, trans. Richard Howard, 1966, p. 46.

4. E. M. Forster's chapter on "The Plot" in *Aspects of the Novel*.

5. Muriel Bradbrook, *Themes and Conventions in Elizabethan Tragedy*.

6. Bergson, *Creative Evolution*, trans. Arthur Mitchell, 1924, p. 330.

7. Frederick Turner in *Shakespeare and the Nature of Time*, p. 34, comments on Jaques's external vision of life with his emphasis on "the mask, the actor's part. . . . He describes behaviour, but not experience." R. D. Laing in *The Politics of Experience* also distinguishes between behavior and experience.

8. Ricardo J. Quinones in *The Renaissance Discovery of Time* (pp. 134–135) finds that time in Petrarch and his followers "forces a profound personal reassessment" involving a conversion from an aesthetic to an ethical view.

9. See Bergson's essay on *Laughter*.

10. Jaspers, *Man in the Modern Age*, trans. Eden and Cedar Paul, 1957, p. 98.

IV. *Punctual Time: Hamlet*

1. In discussing the clock I have relied on H. Alan Lloyd, "Timekeepers—an Historical Sketch" in: Fraser, *The Voices of Time*, and also on Joseph Needham's article on "Time and Knowledge in China and the West" in the same anthology. Quinones bases his discussion on the principle that "For the men of the Renaissance, time is a great discovery."

2. As noted, in this instance Claudius exhibits, like Hamlet, a delayed response. It is not until IV, 1, that Claudius remarks, "My soul is full of discord and dismay." But see also, III, i, 50 and III, iii, 40.

3. Frederick Turner points out that at the close of the play Hamlet learns to act "with, not against, the current of Time," waiting patiently and surrendering in a relation of "harmony with the present moment." (Turner, *Shakespeare*, pp. 94, 172)

V. *Duration: Macbeth*

1. Aspects of this condensation of time in *Macbeth* are discussed in B. L. Reid, *Tragic Occasions*.

2. Philip Vellacott, *Sophocles and Oedipus*, 1971.

3. The retrospective view is treated in C. B. Purdom, *What Happens in Shakespeare*.

VI. *Patience: Othello*

1. See Fraser, *The Voices of Time*, p. 138, and also Joost A. M. Meerloo, "The Time Sense in Psychiatry," p. 249, in the same anthology.
2. *Ibid.*, pp. 137–138, quoting John A. Kouwenhoven.
3. *Ibid.*, p. 138, quoting Robert H. Knapp.
4. In Mill's essay, "A Few Words on Non-Intervention."
5. Frederick Turner mentions the clash between "two rhythms, two time-schemes" in Iago and Othello (p. 116 f.)

VII. *Space, Time, and Duty: Troilus and Cressida*

1. Satosi Watanabe, "Time and the Probabilistic View of the World," in: Fraser, *Voices of Time*, p. 563.
2. "The Time Sense in Psychiatry" in: *ibid.*, p. 236.
3. *Notebooks*, ed. Irma A. Richter (World's Classics), pp. 263, 273.
4. Frederick Turner calls it "Shakespeare's most diagrammatic and theoretical play" (Turner, *Shakespeare*, p. 108).
5. *Revolt of the Masses*, 1932, p. 34.
6. Frederick Turner (*Shakespeare*, pp. 76, 100) holds that there is "no spiritual freedom" in this play, but seems not to see that Hector is free in the sense that "personal constancy is perhaps our only defence against time."
7. *The Myth of Sisyphus*.
8. Norman Rabkin, *Shakespeare and the Common Understanding*, p. 53.
9. See the closing remarks in Satosi Watanabe, "Time and the Probabilistic View of the World" in: Fraser, *The Voices of Time*, pp. 560–563.

VIII. *The Extremity of Time: Lear*

1. The following explanation is drawn from Joseph Whitehill, "Samuel Taylor Coleridge: Prisoner and Prophet of System," *The American Scholar*, (Winter, 1967–1968). Rudolf Arnheim, *Entropy and Art*, 1971, is also relevant.
2. J. Bronowski in *The Identity of Man* (Chapter 2) discusses how the purpose of scientific statement is to expel ambiguities, whereas poetry can accommodate ambiguities. Bronowski is actually rephrasing the point made by Robert Penn Warren.
3. Richard Schlegel, "Time and Thermodynamics" in: Fraser, *Voices of Time*, p. 504.
4. *Ibid.*, p. 500–501.
5. *Ibid.*, p. 500.

IX. *The Scenic Resolution*

1. Hallett Smith in *Shakespeare's Romances* makes the distinction between theatrical setting and "landscape," which "is described in visual terms but not shown visually on the stage." His book illustrates how in the later plays, especially, Shakespeare creates "landscape" by poetry. A. Richard Turner's *Vision of Landscape* treats "the union of figures and landscape" in painting.

2. Fraser, *Voices of Time*, p. 563.

3. Giulio Carlo Argan, *Fra Angelico*, pp. 22–23.

4. *The Salon of 1859*, the essay on "The Governance of the Imagination."

5. "Et In Arcadia Ego: Poussin and the Elegiac Tradition," in: Panofsky, *Meaning in the Visual Arts*.

Bibliographical Note

Two recent books have discussed in less or greater detail the aspects of time in Shakespearean drama: Frederick Turner's *Shakespeare and the Nature of Time: Moral and Philosophical Themes in Some Plays and Poems of William Shakespeare* and Ricardo J. Quinones's *The Renaissance Discovery of Time*. Turner is primarily concerned with the general effects of time on characters in the plays. The second book makes a thorough investigation of the Renaissance time sense in major writers of the period and provides a magisterial array of evidence how these writers, including Shakespeare, attempted to negate the wastage of time by their ideals of familial succession, fame, and fidelity in love. Quinones firmly establishes the Renaissance context for Shakespeare's Elizabethan responses to time.

Another book of primary importance on Shakespeare's manipulation of time is Emrys Jones's *Scenic Form in Shakespeare*. In his second chapter Jones reviews the many disputes about so-called stretched time (long time and short time) in the plays and comes to the convincing conclusion that Shakespeare does not, except in plays like *Romeo and Juliet*, depend upon clock time but upon a tempo of scenes following each other in a flow of emotional, not chronometric, logic. "Time in the measurable sense," Jones says, "does not enter into the matter." Words like "tomorrow" or "yesterday" provide dramatic movement, not calendar intervals. In sum, Jones understands how Shakespeare relies upon imagined time, not serial moments. Time is a psychic index.

Then there is Hallett Smith's *Shakespeare's Romances: A Study of Some Ways of the Imagination*, recognizing that theatrical setting is not the same as landscape, the "verbal scene painting" that creates psychic atmosphere. Ever since G. Wilson Knight wrote his influential essay on "The Principles of Shakespearian Interpretation" (in *The Wheel of Fire: Interpre-*

tations of Shakespearian Tragedy), this "spatial" analysis has been of increasing interest. Mark Rose in *Shakespearean Design* offers an examination of the structure of Elizabethan drama to show how Shakespeare depends upon Renaissance principles of spatial composition, his scenes ordered in a counterpoint of diptych and triptych patterns within a "frame" or "full circle technique."

The following writers are cited or otherwise referred to in the text:

Argan, Giulio Carlo. *Fra Angelico.* Translated by James Emmons. Geneva [?]: Skira, 1955.

Arnheim, Rudolf. *Entropy and Art: An Essay on Disorder and Order.* Berkeley: University of California Press, 1971.

Artaud, Antonin. *The Theatre and Its Double.* Translated by Mary C. Richards. New York: Grove Press, 1958.

Bachelard, Gaston. *L'Intuition de l'instant.* Paris: Gonthier, 1932.

Bergson, Henri. *Creative Evolution.* Translated by Arthur Mitchell. New York: H. Holt and Company, 1924.

――――. *Time and Free Will.* Translated by R. A. Audran, C. Brereton, and W. H. Carter. 1910. Reprint. Atlantic Highlands, N. J.: Humanities Press, 1971.

――――. *The Two Sources of Morality and Religion.* Translated by R. A. Audra and C. Brereton. 1935. Reprint. Westport, Conn.: Greenwood Press, 1974.

Bradbrook, Muriel. Elizabethan Stage Conditions. 2d ed. Cambridge, England: Cambridge University Press, 1968.

――――. *Shakespeare the Craftsman.* London: Chatto and Windus, 1969.

――――. *Themes and Conventions in Elizabethan Tragedy.* 1935. 2d ed. Cambridge, England: Cambridge University Press, 1952–60.

Bradley, A. C. *Shakespearean Tragedy: Lectures on Hamlet, Othello, King Lear, and Macbeth.* 2d ed. New York: St. Martin's Press, 1956.

Bronowski, Jacob. *The Identity of Man.* Rev. ed. Garden City, N. Y.: Natural History Press, 1971.

Brown, Norman O. *Life Against Death: The Psychoanalytical Meaning of History.* Middletown, Conn.: Wesleyan University Press, 1959.

Buland, Mabel. *The Presentation of Time in the Elizabethan Drama.* 1912. Reprint. New York: Haskell House, 1969.

Caillois, Roger. *Man, Play, and Games.* Translated by M. Barash. New York: Free Press, 1961.

Camus, Albert. *The Myth of Sisyphus and Other Essays.* New York: Alfred A. Knopf, 1955.

Cassirer, Ernst. *Mythical Thought.* Translated by Ralph Manheim. Vol. 2 of *The Philosophy of Symbolic Forms.* New Haven, Conn.: Yale University Press, 1955.

Clark, Kenneth. *Landscape into Art.* 1949. Reprint. Levittown, N. Y.: Transatlantic Arts, 1961.

Collingwood, R. G. *The Idea of History.* Oxford, England: Clarendon Press, 1946.

Cornford, F. M. *From Religion to Philosophy: A Study in the Origins of Western Speculation.* New York: Harper, 1957.

Craig, Hardin. *An Interpretation of Shakespeare.* 1948. Reprint (text edition). Columbia, Missouri: Lucas Brothers, 1966.

De Romilly, Jacqueline. *Time in Greek Tragedy.* Ithaca, N. Y.: Cornell University Press, 1968.

Drew, Philip. *Matthew Arnold and the Passage of Time,* 1969.

Driver, Tom F. *The Sense of History in Greek and Shakespearean Drama.* New York: Columbia University Press, 1960.

Edwards, Philip. *Shakespeare and the Confines of Art.* London: Methuen, 1972.

Ehrenzweig, Anton. *The Hidden Order of Art: A Study in the Psychology of Artistic Imagination.* Berkeley: University of California Press, 1967.

––––––. *The Psycho-analysis of Artistic Vision and Hearing.* 1953. Reprint. San Marino, Calif.: Huntington Library, 1966.

Elton, William R. *King Lear and the Gods.* San Marino, Calif.: Huntington Library, 1966.

Farnham, Willard. *The Mediaeval Heritage of Elizabethan Tragedy.* Reprinted with corrections. New York: Barnes & Noble, 1956.

––––––. *The Shakespearean Grotesque: Its Genesis and Transformations.* New York: Oxford University Press, 1971.

Fergusson, Francis. *The Idea of a Theatre: A Study of Ten Plays.* 2d ed. Princeton, N. J.: Princeton University Press, 1968.

Flatter, Richard. *Shakespeare's Producing Hand.* 1948. Reprint. Philadelphia, Pa.: R. West, 1973.

Foakes, R. A. *Shakespeare—The Dark Comedies to the Last Plays: From Satire to Celebration.* Charlottesville, Va.: University Press of Virginia, 1971.

Forster, E. M. *Aspects of the Novel.* New York: Harcourt Brace, 1954.

Fraisse, Paul. *The Psychology of Time.* Translated by Jennifer Leith. New York: Harper & Row, 1963.

Fraser, J. T. *Of Time, Passion, and Knowledge.* New York: Braziller, 1975.

––––––, ed. *The Voices of Time.* New York: Braziller, 1966.

Frey, Dagobert. *Gotik und Renaissance.* Augsburg, Germany: Dr. B. Filser, 1929.

Frye, Northrop. *Fools of Time: Studies in Shakespearean Tragedy.* Toronto: University of Toronto Press, 1967.

Gombrich, E. H. *Art and Illusion: A Study in the Psychology of Pictorial Presentation*. Vol. 35, Bollingen Series. Princeton, N. J.: Princeton University Press, 1961.

_____. *Meditations on a Hobby Horse and Other Essays on the Theory of Art*. London: Phaidon, 1963.

Gunn, J. Alexander. *The Problem of Time*. London: George Allen & Unwin, 1929.

Hawkes, Terence. *Shakespeare and the Reason: A Study of the Tragedies and the Problem Plays*. Atlantic Highlands, N. J.: Humanities Press, 1965.

Heidegger, Martin. *Being and Time*. Translated by J. Macquarrie and E. Robinson. New York: Harper & Row, 1962.

_____. *Existence and Being*. Edited by Werner Brock. Chicago: Henry Regnery, 1950.

Heilman, Robert B. "The Economics of Iago and Others." *PMLA* 68 (1953): 555–571.

_____. *Tragedy and Melodrama: Versions of Experience*. Seattle: University of Washington Press, 1968.

Henderson, Drayton. "Shakespeare's *Troilus and Cressida*." In *Essays in Dramatic Literature*, edited by Hardin Craig. Princeton, N. J.: Princeton University Press, 1935.

Jaspers, Karl. *Man in the Modern Age*. Translated by Eden and Cedar Paul. Garden City, N. Y.: Doubleday, 1957.

Jones, Emrys. *Scenic Form in Shakespeare*. New York, Oxford University Press, 1971.

Jorgensen, Paul A. *Redeeming Shakespeare's Words*. Berkeley, University of California Press, 1962.

Kitto, H. D. F. *Greek Tragedy: A Literary Study*. 3d ed., rev. London: Methuen, 1966.

Knight, G. Wilson. "The Principles of Shakespearian Interpretation." In *The Wheel of Fire: Interpretations of Shakespearian Tragedy*. London: Methuen, 1962.

Kott, Jan. *Shakespeare Our Contemporary*. Translated by Boleslaw Taborski. New York: W. W. Norton, 1974.

Kubler, George A. *The Shape of Time: Remarks on the History of Things*. New Haven, Conn.: Yale University Press, 1962.

Laing, R. D. *The Politics of Experience*. New York: Ballantine, 1967.

Laporte, Paul. "Art and Alienation." *Centennial Review* 12 (Spring 1968).

Lawlor, John. *The Tragic Sense in Shakespeare*. New York: Harcourt, Brace, 1960.

Leech, Clifford. *Shakespeare's Tragedies and Other Studies in Seventeenth Century Drama*. London: Chatto and Windus, 1950.

———. "The Structure of the Last Plays." *Shakespeare Survey* 11.

Lovejoy, Arthur O. *The Great Chain of Being.* Cambridge, Mass.: Harvard University Press, 1964.

Mack, Maynard. *King Lear in Our Time.* Berkeley: University of California Press, 1971.

———. "The World of Hamlet." *Yale Review* 41 (Summer 1952): 502–23.

Margeson, J. M. R. *The Origins of English Tragedy.* New York: Oxford University Press, 1967.

Ornstein, Robert. *The Moral Vision of Jacobean Tragedy.* 1960. Reprint. Westport, Conn.: Greenwood Press, 1975.

Ortega y Gasset, José. *Revolt of the Masses.* New York: W. W. Norton, 1957.

Panofsky, Erwin. *Meaning in the Visual Arts.* Garden City, N.Y.: Doubleday, 1955.

Peterson, Douglas L. *Time, Tide, and Tempest: A Study of Shakespeare's Romances.* San Marino, Calif.: Huntington Library, 1973.

Piaget, Jean. *The Child's Conception of Time.* Translated by A. J. Pomerans. New York: Basic Books, 1970.

Pickering, F. P. *Literature and Art in the Middle Ages.* Coral Gables, Fla.: University of Miami Press, 1970.

Poulet, Georges. *Studies in Human Time.* Translated by Elliott Coleman. Baltimore, Md.: Johns Hopkins Press, 1956.

Prezzolini, Giuseppe. *Machiavelli.* Translated by Gioconda Savine. New York: Farrar, Straus & Giroux, 1967.

Pucelle, Jean. *Le Temps.* Paris: Presses Universitaires de France, 1959.

Puech, Henri-Charles. "Gnosis and Time." *Eranos Yearbooks* 3 (1957).

Purdom, C. B. *What Happens in Shakespeare.* London: J. Baker, 1963.

Quinones, Ricardo J. *The Renaissance Discovery of Time.* Cambridge, Mass.: Harvard University Press, 1972.

Rabkin, Norman. *Shakespeare and the Common Understanding.* New York: Free Press, 1967.

Reid, B. L. *Tragic Occasions: Essays on Several Forms.* Port Washington, N. Y.: Kennikat Press, 1971.

Ribner, Irving. *The English History Play in the Age of Shakespeare.* Princeton, N.J.: Princeton University Press, 1957. Rev. ed. New York: Barnes & Noble, 1965.

Richter, Irma A., ed. *The Notebooks of Leonardo da Vinci.* New York: Oxford University Press, 1952.

Robbe-Grillet, Alain. *La Maison de Rendez-Vous.* Translated by Richard Howard. New York: Grove Press, 1966.

Rose, Mark. *Shakespearean Design.* Cambridge, Mass.: Belknap Press, Harvard University Press, 1972.

Roupnel, Gaston. *Nouvelle Siloë*. Paris: Editions B. Grasset, 1945.

Salingar, Leo. *Shakespeare and the Traditions of Comedy*. New York: Cambridge University Press, 1974.

Schrödinger, Erwin. *What is Life? and Other Scientific Essays*. Garden City, N. Y.: Doubleday, 1956.

Smith, Hallett. *Shakespeare's Romances: A Study of Some Ways of the Imagination*. San Marino, Calif.: Huntington Library, 1972.

Stampfer, Judah Leon. "Ideas of Order in Shakespeare's Histories and Tragedies." Ph.D. dissertation, Harvard University, 1959.

Tillyard, E. M. W. *The Elizabethan World Picture*. 1943. Reprint. New York: Vintage Books, Random House, 1959.

Toulmin, Stephen, and Goodfield, June. *The Discovery of Time*. New York: Harper & Row, 1965.

Turner, A. Richard. *The Vision of Landscape in Renaissance Italy*. 2d ed. Princeton, N. J.: Princeton University Press, 1974.

Turner, Frederick. *Shakespeare and the Nature of Time: Moral and Philosophical Themes in Some Plays and Poems of William Shakespeare*. New York: Oxford University Press, 1971.

Valéry, Paul. *History and Politics*. Translated by Denise Folliot and Jackson Mathews. Vol. 45, Bollingen Series. New York: Pantheon Books, 1962.

Vellacott, Philip. *Sophocles and Oedipus*. Ann Arbor, Mich.: University of Michigan Press, 1971.

Watson, Curtis B. *Shakespeare and the Renaissance Concept of Honor*. Princeton, N. J.: Princeton University Press, 1960.

Weiss, Theodore. *The Breath of Clowns and Kings: A Book on Shakespeare*. New York: Atheneum, 1971.

Whitehead, Alfred North. *Science and the Modern World*. 1925. Reprint. New York: Free Press, 1967.

Whitehill, Joseph. "Samuel Taylor Coleridge: Prisoner and Prophet of System." *The American Scholar* 37 (Winter 1967–68)

Wittkower, Rudolf. *Architectural Principles in the Age of Humanism*. Reprint. New York: W. W. Norton, 1971.

Zeeveld, W. Gordon. *The Temper of Shakespeare's Thought*. New Haven, Conn.: Yale University Press, 1974.